the **higgidy** cookbook

the higgidy cookbook

100 recipes for pies and more

camilla stephens

Quercus

contents

A note from Camilla
founder of Higgidy

From a very young age I loved to cook. Late at night I would secretly read cookbooks by torchlight under my duvet, but I never imagined the journey my love of food would take me on. I could never have predicted I would start a pie company, nor did I dare to dream I'd get the opportunity to write a cookery book of my own.

Along the way, I've discovered so much about food. I've learnt that food can be fun, that it nurtures, comforts and sustains. Food brings people together – it's for sharing and celebrating; and, above all, it brings colour to our lives. Mealtimes for me are often the brightest moments in my day, eagerly anticipated, to be savoured, shared and enjoyed. I hope this book can help make every mealtime colourful.

As a mum juggling family and work, I know how daunting it can be putting a meal on the table, coaxing children into trying new foods and keeping cooking fun and interesting. So in this book you'll find plenty of simple suppers that can be made quickly after work or prepared ahead and popped in the oven just before serving. I hope some of these pages will soon become sticky with buttery fingerprints!

I also show how to use different types of pastry to make quiches, tarts, baskets, vol-au-vents, tartlets and even a frying-pan pie. Lots of our pies will feel familiar – a little bit like putting on a favourite cosy jumper – while others may surprise you. Traditional favourites like Quiche Lorraine sit alongside fun and more unusual creations, including a whole chapter of party pies, from a beautiful Wedding Pie to my Little Hot Dog Rolls, which can be made ahead and served straight from the oven as quirky canapés. Some of these recipes do take a little more thought and effort but you can carry the results to the table with a proud glow and enjoy the murmur of 'wows' from all who dig in.

Towards the back of the book I share my tips for perfect pastry, including recipes for different types and flavours and useful secrets that I've learnt along the way. There are also yummy ideas for side dishes to serve with the main event.

But for me, it was the pudding pies and sweet treats that were the most fun to write. I'm not going to apologise for the number of times my daughter and I licked out the bowl or enjoyed 'testing' the fudgy middle or sticky crunchy edges of a sweet gooey tart fresh from the oven.

So there's nothing left to say except be brave and be proud!
A homemade meal arriving on a table is one of life's greatest gifts.

A few little cooking notes to help you along the way...

❧ We recommend using free-range eggs, poultry and meat for all our recipes. It's better not to use them straight from the fridge but to let them come to room temperature first.

❧ All onions and garlic should be peeled, unless otherwise directed. Try not to be too brutal when cooking them; cook gently unless the recipe specifically directs a sizzling-hot flame!

❧ If using ready-made stock, choose a good-quality one for the best results and most balanced flavour.

❧ Where herbs are called for, we really do recommend using fresh herbs. The ones in jars just aren't as good.

❧ For recipes requiring citrus zest, it's best to use unwaxed fruit. But if you can't get hold of this, wash waxed fruits thoroughly in warm soapy water before use.

❧ 1 teaspoon = 5ml; 1 tablespoon = 15ml. All spoon measures are level unless otherwise specified.

❧ Oven temperatures are given in degrees Celsius, with the equivalents for fan-assisted and gas ovens. But remember that all ovens do vary, so use our timings as a guide and always keep an eye on your cooking. (An oven thermometer is a great investment for pie-making!)

❧ And finally, it's worth getting yourself as organised as possible so that you can enjoy the meal, your guests or that special occasion. Do as much preparation in advance as you dare and leave the final bake or stage of assembly for when you are ready to eat.

And a little note about tins, pie dishes and funnels

Each recipe in this book indicates the size of pie dish or tin needed for baking. In most cases we haven't stated the exact material the container might be made of because we think it's a little daft having to rush out and buy something specially. If you are lucky enough to have a deep cupboard filled with all sorts of cooking pots and baking tins, here are some tips:

❧ Bake double-crust pies in metallic or enamel pie tins, as they conduct the heat better than ceramic dishes.

❧ Deep ceramic dishes are good for pies that only have a pastry lid, but you may well need a pie funnel. This acts a bit like a chimney, allowing steam to escape from the hot filling so that it doesn't bubble up through the pastry. A funnel also provides support for the lid, helping to prevent it sagging or losing its shape. The funnel is placed in the middle of the uncooked pie with its top poking up through the pastry. You can buy fun, decorative funnels that add to the drama of your finished pie!

❧ For quiches and tarts, loose-bottomed tins are great. They allow a lovely even bake and make it easy to remove the tin before showing off your work of art at the table.

❧ Sweet fruit pies and cobblers work best in shallower dishes or pie plates, allowing you to cut generous wedges, and making it more likely that the pastry at the centre of the dish gets cooked right through.

simple suppers

pea and parmesan parcels

MAKES 6 PARCELS
250g frozen petits pois
4 spring onions, finely chopped
50g blanched almonds,
 roughly chopped
1 medium egg, beaten
100g cream cheese
100g feta cheese, crumbled
50g Parmesan cheese,
 finely grated
6 sheets of filo pastry
75g butter, melted
About 30 fresh mint leaves
Sea salt and freshly ground
 black pepper

We're rather partial to peas at Higgidy – it might sound a bit childish, but we've been known to have little more for supper than a huge bowl of peas with a knob of melted butter and some sea salt! So in honour of this fondness we've devised a pastry parcel around the humble pea.

1 Preheat the oven to 200°C/fan 180°C/gas mark 6. Put the petits pois, spring onions, almonds, beaten egg, cream cheese, feta and Parmesan into a big bowl and mix well. It's easiest to do this with your hands to make sure all the ingredients are thoroughly combined. Season well with salt and pepper.

2 Lay a sheet of filo on your work surface and brush it with melted butter. Place 10 whole mint leaves randomly on top and sandwich with a second sheet of filo. Brush again with melted butter. Cut your double-thickness filo in half, lengthways, to give you two oblongs.

3 Starting at one end of an oblong, spoon one-sixth of the filling mixture on to the filo towards a corner. Fold over the corner with the filling on it diagonally to form a triangle. Continue to fold in this way, retaining the triangle shape. Repeat with the second oblong.

4 Now repeat steps 2 and 3 with the next two sheets of filo and half the remaining filling, then with the last two sheets and the rest of the filling so that you have six triangles.

5 Place the triangles on a cold baking tray that's lined with non-stick baking paper. Brush with the remaining butter and sprinkle with sea salt. Bake in the oven for 20 minutes or until golden and crisp.

sausage and bean pie with ciabatta crumbs

SERVES 4

Equipment: 1 x 2.5–3-litre
shallow ovenproof casserole pan

1 quantity of Spiced Tomato
  Sauce (see page 203)
4 tbsp olive oil
8 good-quality Toulouse sausages
150g chorizo cooking sausage,
  sliced
1 x 400g tin of cannellini beans,
  drained and rinsed
1 small bunch of fresh flat-leaf
  parsley, leaves chopped
140g ciabatta bread,
  torn into pieces
Zest of 1 lemon, grated
  or peeled with a zester
Salt

The secret to success with this recipe is the lovely spiced tomato sauce and using good-quality Toulouse sausages. It's quick to fling together and you can even use slightly stale bread. We bet this one becomes a family favourite.

1 Make the spiced tomato sauce according to the method on page 203. Preheat the oven to 200°C/fan 180°C/gas mark 6.

2 Heat 2 tablespoons of olive oil in your casserole pan over a medium–high heat. Add the sausages and brown them all over, then add the chorizo and fry for a minute or two, or until starting to crisp at the edges. At this stage your sausages won't be fully cooked through, but that's okay. Add the beans, half the parsley and the tomato sauce.

3 Pulse the torn ciabatta in a food processor for just a few seconds or until it forms rough breadcrumbs. Stir in the remaining oil, half the remaining parsley, half the lemon zest and a little salt.

4 Pile the crumb mixture on top of the sausage mixture, spread out evenly and bake in the oven for 35–40 minutes or until the crust is golden and the sausages are cooked through. Cover with foil if it starts to brown too much. Once cooked, sprinkle with the remaining parsley and lemon zest and serve.

summery pizza pie

SERVES 8

1 quantity of Savoury Croustade
   Pastry (see page 217)
A little plain flour, for dusting

For the filling:
A knob of butter
3 garlic cloves, roughly chopped
200g baby courgettes (approx. 6),
   cut into 1.5cm slices on an angle
4 large spring onions, cut into
   1.5cm slices on an angle
75g samphire, washed and any
   large pieces halved (or use
   asparagus spears instead)
250g full-fat cream cheese
1 medium egg
Zest of 1 lemon, grated
   or peeled with a zester
2 tbsp chopped fresh
   flat-leaf parsley
Salt and freshly ground
   black pepper

For the topping:
1 ball of buffalo mozzarella, torn
A little beaten egg, for brushing
Finely grated zest of ½ a lemon

Samphire is a sea vegetable that likes growing on mud flats – one place we've found it is while foraging on the north Norfolk coast. It can also sometimes be bought from fishmongers and supermarkets, when in season. It has a crisp texture and tastes of the sea. It's good cooked very simply, in butter, but here we've used it on top of our summery pizza pie. If you can't get hold of it, asparagus is just as delicious.

1 Make the croustade pastry according to the method on page 217 and put it into the fridge to rest for 30 minutes.

2 Melt the butter in a large frying pan. When it's sizzling, throw in the garlic and courgettes and fry over a high heat for 2 minutes. Add the spring onions and samphire (or asparagus) and fry for a further 4 minutes or until the veg is beginning to steam but hasn't lost its vibrant colour. Set aside to cool.

3 Beat the egg in a medium bowl and then beat in the cream cheese until fully incorporated. Season with black pepper. Add two-thirds of the cooled vegetables, the lemon zest and chopped parsley and stir to combine. Preheat the oven to 200°C/fan 180°C/gas mark 6.

4 On a lightly floured surface, roll out the pastry into a 30cm circle, about 3mm thick. Transfer to a large baking sheet (the pastry may hang over the sides). Spoon the creamy mixture on to the pastry, leaving a border of about 5cm all the way round the edge. Sprinkle over one-third of the torn mozzarella and a good grating of black pepper (and a pinch of salt if using asparagus). Top with the remaining vegetables and mozzarella. Turn up the excess pastry around the edges of the filling.

5 Brush any exposed pastry with beaten egg and bake for about 25 minutes or until the pastry is golden and crisp. Remove from the oven and sprinkle with a little fresh lemon zest. Allow to sit for 5–10 minutes before slicing into wedges.

wintry pizza pie

SERVES 8

1 quantity of Savoury Croustade
  Pastry (see page 217)
A little plain flour, for dusting

For the filling:
10 shallots, halved
300g parsnips (approx. 3), peeled
  and cut into 2–3cm chunks
1 tbsp olive oil
2 tbsp maple syrup
100g vacuum-packed cooked
  chestnuts, roughly chopped
250g full-fat cream cheese
1 medium egg, beaten
Salt and freshly ground
  black pepper

For the topping:
A little beaten egg, for brushing
100g Stilton cheese, crumbled
1 tbsp chopped fresh rosemary

This is a variation of the summery pizza pie, using blue cheese, roasted parsnips and sweet, sticky chestnuts. It's a really warming take on a pizza and is perfect for a simple pre-Christmas dinner.

1 Make the croustade pastry according to the method on page 217 and put it in the fridge to rest for 30 minutes.

2 Preheat the oven to 200°C/fan 180°C/gas mark 6. Put the shallots, parsnips, olive oil and maple syrup into a small roasting tin and shake it a little, to coat all the vegetables. Pop in the oven for 30 minutes or until the parsnips have softened and everything is lovely and golden. Remove from the oven, stir in the chestnuts and allow to cool completely.

3 In a medium bowl beat the egg and then beat in the cream cheese until fully incorporated. Season with a little salt and black pepper. Add two-thirds of the cooled vegetable mixture and stir to combine, then set aside.

4 On a lightly floured work surface, roll out the pastry into a 30cm circle, about 3mm thick. Transfer to a large baking sheet (the pastry may hang over the sides). Spoon the creamy mixture on to the pastry, leaving a border of about 5cm all the way round the edge. Sprinkle over one-third of the crumbled Stilton and a good grinding of black pepper. Top with the remaining vegetables and sprinkle over the rest of the Stilton and the rosemary. Turn up the sides of the pastry around the edges of the filling.

5 Brush any exposed pastry with beaten egg and bake for about 25 minutes or until the pastry is golden and crisp. Remove from the oven and allow to sit for 5–10 minutes before slicing into wedges.

venison sausage pies with parmesan mash

SERVES 4

Equipment: 4 x shallow ovenproof dishes, about 13cm in diameter, or 1 x 2-litre pie dish

1 tbsp olive oil
8 venison sausages
125g smoked bacon lardons
250g mixed portabella and
   chestnut mushrooms,
   thickly sliced
2 knobs of butter
1 large white onion, thinly sliced
1 large garlic clove, finely chopped
1 tbsp plain flour
150ml red wine (or replace with
   beef stock if feeding children)
200ml hot beef stock
1 tbsp redcurrant jelly
400g floury potatoes, peeled
   and cut into chunks
250g celeriac, peeled and
   cut into chunks
A generous splash of milk
   or single cream
20g Parmesan cheese, finely grated
Salt and freshly ground
   black pepper

> **Tip**
> You can make the sausage stew a day or two ahead (or even earlier and freeze it) but bring it up to simmering point before using it in your pie.

Venison is a lean meat that can become dry when cooked, but you can avoid this with venison sausages because they also contain pork belly, which keeps them moist. Combined with onions, garlic, red wine, redcurrant jelly and creamy mash, these are really warming pies.

1 Heat the oil in a large pan over a medium heat. Add the sausages and brown all over, then remove with a slotted spoon to a plate. Add the bacon and mushrooms to the pan and fry until golden, then remove to the plate with the sausages.

2 Add a knob of butter and the onion to the pan and cook for 7 minutes or until soft and golden. Stir in the garlic and cook for 1 minute, then add the flour and cook, stirring, for a minute more.

3 Return the mushrooms, sausages and bacon to the pan. Pour over the wine and let it bubble until reduced by half. Now pour over the stock, cover with a lid, turn down the heat and simmer gently for 25 minutes. Uncover, stir in the redcurrant jelly and simmer for a final 5 minutes.

4 Meanwhile, place the potatoes and celeriac in a large saucepan, cover with cold water and season with salt. Bring to the boil, then reduce the heat and simmer for 15 minutes or until really tender. Drain well, then return the vegetables to the pan and mash with the remaining knob of butter, the milk or cream, half the Parmesan, and salt and pepper to taste.

5 Preheat the grill to high. Pile the hot sausage stew into your four dishes or one large pie dish. Cover with a generous heap of hot creamy mash and sprinkle on the remaining Parmesan. Place under the grill for 5–8 minutes or until golden.

spiced fish pies with coconut hats

SERVES 4 GENEROUSLY
Equipment: 4 x 500ml soup bowls

A little plain flour, for dusting
500g all-butter puff pastry
1 tbsp olive oil
1 large onion, finely chopped
1 tsp dried chilli flakes
1 tsp black mustard seeds
½ tsp ground turmeric
2 tsp cumin seeds
1 tsp ground coriander
600g tinned chopped tomatoes
1 red pepper, deseeded and sliced
1½ tbsp light muscovado
    or other soft brown sugar
Juice of 1 lemon
400ml hot vegetable stock
1 medium egg, beaten
50–60g dried coconut slices
150g basmati rice, rinsed
500g sustainable white fish fillets,
    such as hake or pollock,
    skinned, boned and cubed
200ml coconut milk
1 small bunch of fresh coriander,
    leaves chopped
Salt and freshly ground
    black pepper

This is a brilliant midweek, not-much-time-on-your-hands recipe. Don't be put off by the long ingredients list; the lion's share are likely already in your cupboard and, more importantly, the pies are absolutely delicious.

1 On a lightly floured work surface, roll out the pastry to about 3mm thick. Cut out four rounds, each 1cm larger in diameter than your bowls, and put on a baking sheet lined with non-stick baking paper. Chill in the fridge for 20 minutes.

2 Meanwhile, heat the oil in a large saucepan over a low heat. Add the onion and soften for 5 minutes. Stir in the spices and cook, stirring, for a couple more minutes. Now tip in the chopped tomatoes, bring to a light bubble and stir in the red pepper, sugar, lemon juice and stock. Season well with salt and pepper, then bring to the boil and simmer for 10 minutes.

3 Preheat the oven to 200°C/fan 180°C/gas mark 6. Brush your pastry rounds with beaten egg and top each one with some slices of coconut. Bake in the oven for 15 minutes or until well risen and golden.

4 To cook the basmati rice, place in a saucepan, cover with 300ml of cold water and season with salt. Bring to the boil, then turn the heat to low, cover the pan with a lid and simmer for 10 minutes or until the water has been absorbed and the rice is tender.

5 Add the fish to the tomato sauce and continue to cook for 3 minutes. Stir in the coconut milk and the cooked rice and simmer for a final 4 minutes, to warm through. Check the seasoning, adjusting to taste, and stir in the chopped coriander. Spoon into warmed soup bowls and top each with a coconut pastry hat. Serve immediately.

pork and apple stroganoff pie with cheddar crust

SERVES 6

*Equipment: 1 x 1.4-litre
ovenproof pie dish*

For the Cheddar pastry:
230g plain flour, plus
   a little extra for dusting
½ tsp salt
125g butter, chilled and diced
40g mature Cheddar cheese,
   finely grated
1 medium egg, lightly beaten
2–3 tbsp ice-cold water

For the filling:
1–2 tbsp vegetable oil
A good knob of butter
1 large onion, thinly sliced
1 medium leek, thinly sliced
2 garlic cloves, finely chopped
600g pork tenderloin,
   cut into 2–3cm pieces
2 eating apples, such as
   Braeburn, peeled, cored
   and cut into small wedges
2 tbsp plain flour
200ml cider
1 tbsp grainy mustard
150ml full-fat soured cream
150ml hot chicken stock
Salt and freshly ground
   black pepper

Pork tenderloin, apples, cider and cream are quick to throw together for this pie. We think the Cheddar crust is a perfect match for the filling, but if you're in a rush you can use ready-made savoury shortcrust or even just make the stroganoff on its own and serve it with a rice pilaff.

1 To make the pastry, sift the flour and salt into a food processor. Add the chilled butter and pulse until the mixture looks like fine breadcrumbs. Stir in the cheese, then add the ice-cold water, just enough to bring the pastry together. Shape into a round disc, wrap in clingfilm and put into the fridge to chill for 30 minutes.

2 Meanwhile, make the filling. Heat a tablespoon of oil with the butter in a large non-stick pan, add the onion and leek, and cook gently for 5 minutes to soften the vegetables. Add the garlic and cook for 2 minutes. Spoon into your pie dish.

3 Increase the heat, add a splash more oil, then fry the pork for a couple of minutes only, just enough to brown the meat. Spoon into the pie dish. Keep the pan on a high heat and fry the apple pieces in the remaining fat, until lightly browned and beginning to soften. Transfer to the pie dish. Sprinkle the flour over the top and stir well, to evenly combine.

4 Pour the cider into the empty pan and bubble until reduced by half. Lower the heat, add the mustard, soured cream and stock, and stir well to combine. Season with salt and pepper to taste and immediately pour over the meat in the pie dish. Give it all a good stir and set aside to cool completely.

recipe continues

5 Preheat the oven to 200°C/fan 180°C/gas mark 6. Brush the edges of the pie dish with beaten egg.

6 On a lightly floured work surface, roll out the pastry to about 3mm thick and drape it over the top of the filling. Crimp the edges to seal (see page 210). Cut a steam hole in the middle.

7 Decorate the top of the pastry with your pastry trimmings (cut into apple shapes or leaves) and brush the pie all over with beaten egg. Bake in the oven for 40 minutes or until the filling is piping hot and the pastry is golden and crisp. Serve with wilted kale.

simple fish pie

Equipment: 1 x 1.8-litre ovenproof pie dish

1kg floury potatoes, peeled
    and cut into rough chunks
60ml semi-skimmed milk
2 tbsp olive oil
1 medium onion, finely chopped
300ml white wine (or replace
    with hot fish or vegetable stock
    if cooking for children)
300ml double cream
125g Parmesan cheese, grated
A handful of fresh flat-leaf
    parsley, leaves roughly chopped
450g salmon fillet, skinned,
    boned and cut into chunks
250g coley fillet, skinned,
    boned and cut into chunks
100g frozen peas
Juice of 1 small lemon
60g mature Cheddar
    cheese, grated
Salt and freshly ground
    black pepper

This recipe goes down as happily with children as it does at a smart grown-up dinner – though you might want to leave out the wine and reduce the seasoning if making it for little ones. Coley is not quite as well known as some white fish but it's delicious, and the good thing is that there are plenty swimming around in our seas.

1 First, make your mash. Cook the potatoes in boiling salted water for 12–14 minutes or until tender enough to be cut like soft butter. Drain well and return to the pan, then cover with a lid and shake well so that they break up a little. Mash with the milk and plenty of salt and pepper until there are no more lumps. Set aside to cool.

2 Preheat the oven to 200°C/fan 180°C/gas mark 6. Heat the olive oil in a large frying pan, add the onion and fry for about 10 minutes or until soft and just turning golden.

3 Pour over the wine (or stock) and allow it to bubble for 3–4 minutes or until the liquid has reduced by at least half. Pour in the cream and bring just to the boil, then remove from the heat and stir in the grated Parmesan and chopped parsley. Set aside and allow to cool slightly.

4 Pour the sauce into your ovenproof dish and shake to distribute evenly. Place the fish chunks on top, along with the frozen peas. Squeeze over the lemon juice and gently toss everything together. Spoon on the mash and sprinkle with the grated cheese, then put the dish on a baking sheet and bake in the oven for 35 minutes or until golden and bubbling.

a hearty higgidy hotpot

SERVES 6

Equipment: 1 x 3-litre shallow, lidded ovenproof casserole pan

2 tbsp olive oil, plus
    a little extra for drizzling
600g lamb leg or neck,
    cut into 2–3cm pieces
2 tbsp plain flour
2 onions, sliced
350g carrots, peeled and
    cut into thick slices
2 leeks, sliced
330ml Guinness or stout
450ml lamb stock
100g pearl barley
2 fresh or dried bay leaves
A handful of fresh thyme and
    flat-leaf parsley, leaves chopped
300–400g waxy potatoes, left
    unpeeled and thinly sliced
40g butter
Salt and freshly ground
    black pepper

For stew and potato lovers, this hotpot is hard to beat. Meltingly tender lamb and veggies in a rich gravy, topped simply with sliced potatoes, make this a great one-pot pie.

1 Preheat the oven to 190°C/fan 170°C/gas mark 5.

2 Heat the oil in your casserole pan over a high heat. Season the flour with a generous pinch of salt and pepper. Toss the lamb in the seasoned flour and brown it on all sides. You may find it easier to do this in two batches. Remove the meat with a slotted spoon on to a plate and set to one side.

3 Reduce the heat to medium, then add the onions to the pan with a splash more oil if needed and cook for 5 minutes, to soften. Add the carrots and leeks and put the browned lamb back into the casserole pan. Stir everything together. Pour over the Guinness (or stout) and stock, and stir in the pearl barley and herbs.

4 Cover the filling with a layer of potatoes, overlapping the slices. Break the butter into small knobs, dot all over the potatoes and season with salt and pepper.

5 Cover tightly with the lid and cook in the centre of the oven for 1 hour, then uncover and continue to bake for 35 minutes or until the potatoes are golden and the lamb is tender. Spoon into bowls and devour. We don't think it needs anything else, but if you fancy something green with it try the Petits Pois and Pancetta (see page 195).

chicken and chorizo with spiced paprika crumble

SERVES 4–6
Equipment: 1 x 2-litre ovenproof pie dish

For the filling:
1 tbsp olive oil
100g chorizo cooking sausage, sliced into 5mm rounds
2 red onions, roughly chopped
3 garlic cloves, finely chopped
250g floury potatoes, peeled and diced
2 tbsp plain flour
450ml hot chicken stock
150ml single cream
1 cooked chicken (approx. 1kg) from a deli counter, skin removed and flesh torn into large pieces
Grated zest of 1 lemon
2 tbsp lemon juice
75g young spinach leaves, roughly chopped
Salt and freshly ground black pepper

For the crumble:
75g plain flour
100g dried breadcrumbs
40g Parmesan cheese, freshly grated
1 tsp smoked paprika
75g butter, chilled and diced

This is such a super-speedy recipe. Chorizo complements the chicken with its strong, smoky flavour and adds some fantastic colour. We've topped it with a spiced crumble that soaks up some of the delicious juices and makes a fine alternative to a puff pastry lid.

1 Preheat the oven to 200°C/fan 180°C/gas mark 6.

2 Heat the olive oil in a large, deep-sided, heavy-based pan with a lid. Add the chorizo, onions and garlic and cook over a high heat for 4–5 minutes or until the onions begin to caramelise and the chorizo starts to release its oil.

3 Add the diced potatoes and cook for 2 minutes. Add the flour and stir to combine, then pour in the chicken stock and give the mixture a good stir. Reduce the heat to low and simmer, covered with the lid, for 20 minutes. You may need to stir the sauce after 10 minutes to stop the mixture catching on the bottom of the pan.

4 Remove from the heat and stir in the cream. Pour into a large bowl and add the chicken pieces. Mix to combine then stir in the lemon zest, lemon juice and raw chopped spinach. Season with salt and pepper and set aside.

5 Now prepare the crumble. Place all the ingredients in a large bowl. Using your fingertips, rub in the butter until the mixture resembles breadcrumbs. (Or you can do this more quickly in a food processor.)

6 Spoon the chicken filling into your pie dish and sprinkle over the crumble. Bake in the oven for 30 minutes and serve piping hot!

feel-good chicken and mushroom pie

This is a lighter pie for those of us watching that waistline! There's heat from the chilli, flavour from the coriander and soy sauce, and heartiness from the beans, all hidden under a crispy veil of filo pastry.

SERVES 6
Equipment: 1 x 2-litre ovenproof pie dish

For the stock:
1 small free-range chicken (1.25kg)
1 celery stick, roughly chopped
1 carrot, peeled and
  roughly chopped
2 sprigs of fresh rosemary
1 bay leaf
6 peppercorns
1 tsp mustard seeds

For the filling:
30g butter, melted,
  plus a knob for frying
250g chestnut mushrooms,
  sliced
2 garlic cloves, crushed
1 red bird's-eye chilli,
  deseeded and finely chopped
4 spring onions, finely chopped
1 small bunch of fresh coriander,
  leaves roughly chopped
300g tinned beans (a mixture
  of borlotti and cannellini
  is good), drained and rinsed
2 tbsp cornflour
2 tbsp light soy sauce
3–4 sheets of filo pastry
Salt and freshly ground
  black pepper

1 Make the stock by putting the chicken into a large saucepan with the celery, carrot, rosemary, bay leaf and peppercorns. Cover with cold water. Bring to the boil, then reduce the heat and simmer gently for 1¼ hours, skimming off any scum that forms on top. Take the chicken out of the pan and leave to cool.

2 Strain the stock into a clean pan. Bring to the boil, add the mustard seeds and simmer until reduced to about 1 litre. You only need 600ml here, so measure it now (you can freeze the rest). When the chicken is cool enough to handle, remove the skin and cut the meat into bite-sized pieces. Set aside.

3 Melt a knob of butter in a large, deep frying pan over a medium heat. Add the mushrooms, season with salt and pepper, and fry until just browned. Add the garlic and chilli and fry for a further minute. Stir in the spring onions and coriander and remove from the heat. Mix in the beans and chicken pieces. Tip into your ovenproof dish.

4 Preheat the oven to 200°C/fan 180°C/gas mark 6. Mix the cornflour in a small bowl with 2–3 tablespoons of the stock. Stir until completely combined. Pour the rest of the stock into a pan, add the cornflour mixture and soy sauce, then bring to the boil and bubble for a minute or two until slightly thicker and glossy. Pour over the chicken and bean mixture.

5 Melt the 30g of butter in a small pan. Brush a filo sheet with the melted butter and lay it on top of your pie. Brush the other filo sheets with butter, loosely scrunch and place on top of the first layer. Brush any unbuttered bits and bake for 35 minutes or until the filo is golden and crisp, and the filling piping hot.

mince and tattie pies

MAKES 12 FILLED
POTATO HALVES
*Equipment: 1 x 3-litre
ovenproof casserole pan*

6 large baking potatoes
2 tbsp olive oil
500g lean minced beef
2 onions, diced
2 garlic cloves, finely chopped
1 carrot, peeled and diced
200g swede, peeled and diced
2 tbsp plain flour
2 tbsp tomato purée
1 tbsp Worcestershire sauce
500ml hot beef stock
30g butter
50g mature Cheddar
    cheese, grated
Salt and freshly ground black
    pepper (if feeding very small
    children you may want to omit)

This recipe is great for children; they love each getting their own little filled tattie. However, if you don't have time to fill the individual skins, simply put the meat into a large ovenproof dish and top with the mash – same taste, different look!

1 Preheat the oven to 200°C/fan 180°C/gas mark 6. Pierce your potatoes once or twice with a sharp knife, pop on a baking tray and bake for approximately 1½ hours. If they are on the small side, check them a little sooner.

2 Heat half the oil in your casserole pan over a high heat and add the beef. Fry until it begins to break down and become dark brown. Remove from the pan and set aside. Add the remaining oil to the pan with the onions and garlic and fry over a medium heat for a few minutes, then add the carrot and swede. Continue to cook for 4–5 minutes, until the veg is beginning to sweat and take on a little colour.

3 Return the mince to the pan and sprinkle over the flour. Add the tomato purée, Worcestershire sauce and stock. Give it a good stir and add some salt and pepper. Cover with a lid and simmer over a low heat for 20–25 minutes. Set aside.

4 Remove the potatoes from the oven, leaving it turned on, and slice in half horizontally (be careful; they'll be hot!). Using a big spoon, scoop the insides of each potato into a large bowl, retaining the skins. Return the empty skins to the baking tray and pop back in the oven for 5–10 minutes to dry out. Add the butter to the potato in the bowl and mash well to remove the lumps. Season with salt and pepper and set aside.

5 Remove the potato skins from the oven and reduce the temperature to 180°C/fan 160°C/gas mark 4. Fill each potato skin with a good spoonful of mince and top with mashed potato. Sprinkle over a little grated cheese and put back into the oven for 30 minutes, then serve.

chicken pot pie

SERVES 6–8

Equipment: 1 x 2-litre ovenproof pie dish; heart-shaped pastry cutter

45g butter
35ml olive oil
4 large leeks, sliced into fat rounds
2 large shallots, finely diced
   (or an onion will do)
500g free-range chicken meat
   (a mix of breast and thigh),
   chopped into rough chunks
300g good-quality cooked ham,
   roughly chopped
3 sprigs of fresh rosemary, leaves
   stripped and finely chopped
4 sprigs of fresh thyme, leaves
   stripped and finely chopped
2 tbsp plain flour
300ml hot good-quality
   chicken stock
200ml single cream
150g mature Cheddar
   cheese, grated
1 rounded tbsp Dijon mustard
A little plain flour, for dusting
800g all-butter puff pastry
1 medium egg, beaten
Salt and freshly ground
   black pepper

A pot pie is a baked savoury pie completely encased in buttery flaky pastry. This one has become a firm favourite at Higgidy and features regularly on the menu for our summer festival season. We can't reveal the original Higgidy recipe because it's a closely guarded secret, but this is a jolly good version – perfect for sharing with your family at lunchtime.

1 Preheat the oven to 200°C/fan 180°C/gas mark 6.

2 Heat 35g of the butter with the olive oil in a large, deep, heavy-based pan over a medium heat, add the leeks and shallots, stir well and cover. Lower the heat and cook for 7–8 minutes or until the vegetables are soft.

3 Add the chicken and increase the heat. Stir frequently for about 6 minutes or until the chicken is just cooked through. Remove from the heat and add the ham and herbs. Give it all a good stir, then add the flour and stir to coat.

4 Add the stock, stir well and return the pan to the heat. Bring to a gentle simmer and cook for 2–3 minutes, to thicken. Remove from the heat, add the cream, cheese and mustard and stir well. Taste your filling and season with a little salt and black pepper if needed. Leave to cool.

5 Using the remaining butter, lightly grease your ovenproof dish. On a lightly floured work surface, roll out two-thirds

recipe continues ⟶

of the pastry (about 500g) to about 3mm thick and use it to line the dish, letting the pastry drape over the sides. Pile in the cooled filling.

6 Dust the work surface with more flour, then roll out the remaining pastry to about 1cm thick and cover the whole pie with it, allowing the pastry to come just over the edges. Trim away any excess and press the edges together with your fingers to seal, or use the back of a fork. If you've got time and are feeling confident, you can crimp the edges (see page 210). Generously glaze the top with beaten egg.

7 Scrunch up the pastry trimmings and roll them out to about 3mm thick. Cut out some heart shapes and decorate the top of the pie with them, glazing with more beaten egg.

8 Bake the pie on a baking sheet in the oven for 20 minutes, then lower the heat to 180°C/fan 160°C/gas mark 4 and bake for another 20 minutes or until the top is puffy and golden. Serve immediately with a big bowl of garden peas topped with fresh mint and a knob of butter.

roast chicken dinner in a pie

SERVES 4–6

Equipment: 1 x 1.5–1.8-litre ovenproof pie dish

Approx. 220g leftover roast chicken (a mix of breast and leg meat if possible), torn into pieces and skin removed

Approx. 430g mixed leftover roast vegetables (or see tip)

A little plain flour, for dusting

375g all-butter puff pastry

1 medium egg, beaten

For the sauce:

50g butter

50g plain flour

150ml white wine (or use chicken stock if feeding children)

350ml leftover gravy mixed with 150ml water, or 500ml good-quality chicken stock

A few sprigs of fresh thyme, leaves only

75ml double cream or crème fraîche

1 tsp Dijon mustard

For the stuffing balls:

220g sausage meat (or 3 sausages)

3 rashers of rindless streaky bacon, finely chopped

30g fresh white breadcrumbs

A handful of fresh flat-leaf parsley, leaves chopped

Tip

If roasting vegetables from scratch, use 160g carrots, 200g parsnips, 160g leeks and 2 large potatoes, cooked and chopped into chunks.

This pie transforms leftover chicken into a comforting supper. Please don't take the filling quantities too literally – it's about using up leftovers and not letting anything from your Sunday roast go to waste.

1 To make the sauce, melt the butter in a pan over a medium heat, add the flour and stir to a smooth paste. Gradually add the wine, stirring until smooth, then gradually add your gravy or stock. Bubble for a couple of minutes, then remove from the heat and add the thyme, cream and mustard. Stir well, taste and season. Set aside to cool.

2 For the stuffing balls, mix all the ingredients, shape into walnut-sized balls and chill in the fridge until needed.

3 Preheat the oven to 220°C/fan 200°C/gas mark 7. Toss together the leftover roast chicken and cooked vegetables (cut into similar-sized chunks) and tip into your pie dish. Pour over the sauce and stir together. Arrange the stuffing balls on top – you can push them into the mixture a bit but they should poke up to support the pastry.

4 On a lightly floured work surface, roll out the pastry to about 5mm thick. Brush the sides of the dish with beaten egg. Drape the pastry over the filling and trim any excess. Seal the edges well and cut a steam hole in the centre. Scrunch up your pastry trimmings and roll out to about 3mm thick, then cut out decorative shapes and place them on the pie. Brush all over with the remaining beaten egg.

5 Reduce the oven temperature to 200°C/fan 180°C/gas mark 6 and bake for 45 minutes or until the filling is piping hot. Cover with foil if the pastry is browning too quickly.

chinese spiced beef pies

SERVES 4–5
*Equipment: 4–5 x 300ml ovenproof
pie dishes or 1 x 1.2-litre pie dish*

1 quantity of Savoury Shortcrust
    Pastry (see page 212 or use
    ready-made pastry)
1 tbsp olive oil
1 red onion, diced
1 celery stick, diced
1 carrot, peeled and diced
500g minced beef
1 red pepper, deseeded and sliced
2 tsp Chinese five-spice
4cm piece of fresh root ginger,
    peeled and finely chopped
2 large garlic cloves, finely chopped
2 red chillies, deseeded and
    finely chopped
1 x 400g tin of chopped tomatoes
240ml hot beef stock
3 tbsp soy sauce
1 tbsp brown sugar
1 small bunch of fresh coriander,
    leaves chopped
A little plain flour, for dusting
1 medium egg, beaten
1–2 tbsp sesame seeds
Salt and freshly ground
    black pepper

Here, beef mince is cooked with ginger, chilli, spices and soy sauce for a really punchy flavour. The sesame seed lid is a lovely finishing touch. These little pies are great served with some wilted Asian green vegetables.

1 Unless using ready-made, start by making the shortcrust pastry according to the method on page 212. Put it into the fridge to rest for 30 minutes before using.

2 Heat the oil in a large pan over a medium heat, add the onion, celery and carrot and soften for 5 minutes. Add the beef, season with salt and pepper, then turn up the heat and cook until nicely browned, breaking up the mince with a wooden spoon. Add the red pepper, five-spice, ginger, garlic and chillies, mix well and fry for a couple more minutes.

3 Add the tinned tomatoes, stock, soy sauce and sugar. Heat until gently bubbling, then cover with a lid and simmer for 15 minutes. Stir, then simmer for a further 15 minutes, uncovered, to allow the liquid to reduce. Stir in the chopped coriander and spoon the filling into your pie dishes or big dish. Set aside to cool completely.

4 Preheat the oven to 200°C/fan 180°C/gas mark 6. On a lightly floured work surface, roll out the pastry to about 3mm thick and cut out lids (or one large lid) a little larger than your dishes (or dish). Brush the edges of each pie dish with beaten egg, lay the pastry lid on top and seal the edges with your fingers. Brush all over with more beaten egg and sprinkle with sesame seeds. Cut a small steam hole in the centre of each lid.

5 Bake in the oven for 30–35 minutes for individual pies, or 45 minutes for one big pie, or until the pastry is golden and crisp and the filling is piping hot. Some gravy may seep up through the steam hole but this is rather nice and makes the pies look inviting.

spicy tomato and lentil layer pie

SERVES 8

For the walnutty pastry:
400g plain flour,
    plus a little for dusting
½ tsp salt
100g walnuts
60g Parmesan cheese, grated
100g butter, chilled and diced
2 medium eggs, beaten , plus
    a beaten egg for brushing
3 tbsp ice-cold water

For the filling:
½ quantity (about 450g) Spiced
    Tomato Sauce (see page 203)
250g Puy lentils (we like the
    Merchant Gourmet pouches),
    cooked and drained
1 large aubergine
Olive oil, for brushing
200g ricotta cheese
Salt and freshly ground
    black pepper

This is a really tasty vegetarian recipe that can hold its own as a main dish, with layers of aubergine, tomatoey lentils and creamy ricotta cheese all wrapped in a pastry crust. Don't worry about leftovers; this pie is delicious served cold the following day.

1 To make the pastry, pulse the flour, salt, walnuts and Parmesan in a food processor until the ingredients are evenly mixed and the walnuts are finely chopped. Add the butter and pulse again until the mixture resembles breadcrumbs. Add the beaten eggs and ice-cold water and pulse until the mixture just comes together to form a dough, adding a tiny bit more water if you think it's needed.

2 Tip out on to a lightly floured work surface and knead very briefly to bring the pastry together. Don't worry if it's a little crumbly. Divide into two balls, then flatten into discs, wrap in clingfilm and chill in the fridge for 30 minutes.

3 Meanwhile, if you haven't already made the Spiced Tomato Sauce, do so according to the method on page 203 and let it cool down. Stir in the lentils.

4 On a lightly floured work surface, roll out one half of the pastry to about 3mm thick and trim to a 25cm square. Then roll out the other half in the same way, trimming it

recipe continues

to a 30cm square. Put a piece of non-stick baking paper between the layers and return the pastry to the fridge to chill for a further 30 minutes. Don't be tempted to skip this step – it will help prevent any shrinkage in the oven.

5 Cut the aubergine into 5mm slices and brush each one with oil. Fry in a large frying pan over a medium heat until beginning to char and soften. Set aside.

6 Preheat the oven to 200°C/fan 180°C/gas mark 6. Remove your pastry from the fridge and place the smaller piece on a large non-stick baking sheet. Spread the tomato and lentil mixture over it, leaving a 2cm border all the way around. Top with the charred aubergine slices, keeping them away from the edges. Dollop the ricotta over the top, avoiding the edges again, then season generously with salt and pepper.

7 Brush the exposed edges of the base with beaten egg and place the second piece of pastry over the filling, allowing it to droop over the sides. Using the back of a fork, press the pastry edges together to seal. Decorate with pastry shapes if you like. Brush the whole thing with beaten egg and bake on the middle shelf of the oven for 40 minutes or until golden brown.

spiced lamb babotie pie

SERVES 6–8

*Equipment: 1 x 2.5-litre
lidded ovenproof pie dish*

A little butter, for greasing
4 tbsp olive oil
1kg minced lamb
2 onions, finely diced
3 garlic cloves, crushed
2–3 tbsp medium curry powder
   (a little less for children)
¼ tsp ground cinnamon
1 thick slice of slightly stale
   white bread, crusts removed,
   soaked in water for 2 minutes,
   then squeezed dry
3 tbsp tomato purée
Juice and finely grated
   zest of 1 lemon
3 tbsp fruity chutney
1 Bramley or Granny Smith
   apple, peeled, cored and diced
50g dried apricots, chopped
50g raisins
3 bay leaves (optional)
4 medium eggs, lightly beaten
200ml thick natural Greek yoghurt
150ml whole milk
150ml single cream
30g flaked almonds
Salt and freshly ground black pepper

Tip

You can prepare this dish
ahead to the end of step 4,
but you will need to reheat
the meat (covered) so that
it's piping hot before adding
the creamy topping in step 5.

**This classic South African dish looks a lot like moussaka
and has a great combination of spiciness and sweetness.
Despite the long list of ingredients, it's really easy to
make and can be prepared in advance. Serve with a pile
of crispy poppadums or doughy naans, a yoghurty salad
of cucumber, mint and garlic, and some fruity chutneys
(mango is good) and pickles.**

1 Preheat the oven to 160°C/fan 140°C/gas mark 3 and butter
the pie dish. Heat 2 tablespoons of oil in a large pan over a
high heat, add the minced lamb and cook until evenly brown
in colour, stirring all the time. Scoop the mince and any
cooking liquor out of the pan and set aside.

2 Heat the remaining oil in the pan, add the onions and
cook on a medium heat for about 8–10 minutes or until soft.
Add the garlic, curry powder and cinnamon, and cook for
1–2 minutes. Return the meat to the pan and stir in the bread,
tomato purée, lemon juice and zest, chutney, apple, chopped
apricots and raisins. Add 200ml of water and simmer for
10 minutes. Season generously with salt and pepper.

3 Transfer the mixture to your buttered pie dish. Scatter
over the bay leaves. Cover tightly with the lid and bake in
the oven for 1 hour.

4 Remove from the oven, uncover and remove the bay
leaves. If you find residual fat has risen to the surface during
cooking, use kitchen paper to soak it up.

5 Increase the oven heat to 190°C/fan 170°C/gas mark 5.
Mix the eggs, yoghurt, milk and cream with a good pinch
of salt and pepper. Pour over the meat, then scatter with the
almonds. Bake for 15 minutes or until the top is bubbling
and golden brown.

chilli beef pie with spicy potato wedges

SERVES 6
Equipment: 1 x 3-litre lidded ovenproof casserole pan

For the stew:
2 tsp cumin seeds
1–1½ tsp dried chilli flakes
   (depends on how hot you like it!)
1 tsp ground cinnamon
2 tsp dried oregano
750g braising beef, cut into
   4cm pieces, excess fat removed
3 tbsp olive oil
2 onions, finely chopped
3 garlic cloves, finely chopped
1 small bunch of fresh coriander,
   leaves and stalks separated and
   chopped, plus more leaves to serve
2 green chillies, deseeded and diced
2 tbsp tomato purée
200ml red wine (or replace with
   beef stock if feeding children)
1 x 400g tin of chopped tomatoes
2 tbsp black treacle
200ml hot beef stock
1 large red pepper, deseeded
   and diced
1 x 400g tin of black beans,
   drained and rinsed
Salt and freshly ground black pepper

For the wedges:
4 large baking potatoes
2 tbsp olive oil
A good pinch of smoked paprika
A generous handful of grated
   mature Cheddar cheese

This is one of those recipes that cheers the soul. It's pure comfort food, and perfect for a telly supper.

1 Preheat the oven to 180°C/fan 160°C/gas mark 4.

2 Grind the cumin seeds and chilli flakes together with a pestle and mortar, then tip into a large bowl and stir in the cinnamon, oregano and 1 teaspoon of salt. Add the beef and toss to completely coat.

3 Heat a tablespoon of the olive oil in your casserole pan over a medium heat and brown the spiced beef all over in batches, adding more oil if needed. Be careful, because the spices will become bitter if burned. Put the browned beef into a large bowl. Pour a little water into the empty pan, scrape the bottom with a wooden spoon to loosen the spices, then pour this over the beef.

4 In the same pan, heat the remaining oil over a medium heat, then gently fry the onions, garlic, chopped coriander stalks (reserve the chopped leaves) and chillies for 5 minutes or until soft. Add the tomato purée, wine, tinned tomatoes, treacle and stock and stir over a medium heat for a minute or two until well mixed. Add the beef and bring to the boil. As soon as the stew is bubbling, remove from the heat, cover tightly with the lid and cook in the oven for 2 hours.

5 Add the diced pepper and black beans to the pan, give it a good stir, season well with salt and pepper, then put the

recipe continues

lid back on and return to the oven for another 20 minutes. Remove, taste to check the seasoning, and stir in the chopped coriander leaves. Set aside with the lid on tightly.

6 Increase the oven to 200°C/fan 180°C/gas mark 6. Cut the potatoes into chunky wedges and cook in a large pan of boiling water for 8 minutes or until just tender. Drain really well, then tip out on to a shallow roasting tin and drizzle with the oil. Sprinkle over the paprika and some sea salt and bake in the oven for 30 minutes or until crisp and golden. Preheat the grill to medium-high.

7 Now return to your stew, making sure it's still hot – give it a little blast on the hob if necessary. Then scatter the potato wedges over it, top with the grated cheese and pop the dish under the grill, watching until the cheese is melted and bubbling. Garnish with fresh coriander leaves and serve with Fresh Red Salsa (see page 199), soured cream and guacamole on the side.

no-nonsense steak and ale pie

SERVES 6

Equipment: 1 x 3-litre lidded ovenproof casserole pan; 1 x 1.8–2-litre ovenproof pie dish, about 5cm deep

600g braising beef, cut into bite-sized chunks and excess fat removed

2 tbsp plain flour

250g small chestnut mushrooms, thickly sliced

3 garlic cloves, roughly chopped

2 onions, sliced

2 carrots, peeled, halved lengthways and cut into 2–3cm crescents

2 celery sticks, cut into 2–3cm crescents

300ml brown ale

400ml hot beef stock

3 sprigs of fresh thyme, leaves stripped

1 tsp English mustard

Salt and freshly ground black pepper

For the pastry:

A little plain flour, for dusting

375g all-butter puff pastry

1 medium egg, lightly beaten

This recipe is for those who say, 'Wine is fine but beer is better!' It could be pitched as a 'beginner's pie', but you wouldn't guess that from the taste. You need to allow a good few hours for cooking this.

1 Preheat the oven to 180°C/fan 160°C/gas mark 4. Put the braising beef in the casserole pan and sprinkle in the flour. Give it all a good stir, until the flour disappears.

2 Add the mushrooms, garlic, onions, carrots, celery, ale, stock, thyme and mustard. Stir until everything is evenly mixed and season well with salt and pepper. Pop the lid on tightly, and put the stew in the oven for 3 hours, stirring occasionally so it doesn't catch at the bottom.

3 Check the stew a couple of times while it's cooking – you want this to cook slowly, with very little visible 'action' in the pan, just a murmur of bubbles on the surface. If it's bubbling too quickly, reduce the oven temperature. If the level of the liquid is low, add some water and give it a good stir. When ready, remove the stew from the oven and allow to cool completely. Transfer to your pie dish.

4 Turn up the oven to 200°C/fan 180°C/gas mark 6. On a lightly floured work surface, roll out the pastry to a disc just slightly larger than your pie dish, about 3mm thick. Brush the edges of your dish with beaten egg and lay the pastry on top like a tablecloth. Pinch the edges so they stick to the dish and trim off any excess pastry.

5 Cut a hole in the centre for steam to escape and brush the whole pie with beaten egg. Bake in the oven for 35–40 minutes or until the top is crusty and golden brown and the stew is bubbling down below.

giant gruyère and ham sandwich

SERVES 6–8

A little plain flour, for dusting

500g all-butter puff pastry

A little vegetable oil, for greasing

1 tbsp Dijon mustard

3 tbsp crème fraîche

350g good-quality cooked ham, sliced

200g Gruyère cheese, grated

1 medium egg and 1 egg yolk, beaten together

Parmesan cheese, grated, for sprinkling

Ham and cheese is a failsafe combination. This recipe is great for using up any leftover ends of cheese lurking at the back of the fridge, or bits of gammon from a Sunday joint. If feeding children, you can omit the mustard.

1 On a lightly floured work surface, roll out 200g of the puff pastry into a rectangle measuring 25cm x 30cm, and about 3mm thick. Place on a lightly oiled baking sheet and put in the fridge to chill for 20 minutes.

2 Preheat the oven to 220°C/fan 200°C/gas mark 7. Remove the pastry from the fridge and place a second lightly oiled baking sheet directly on top, oiled side touching the pastry (this helps weigh down the pastry to make it crisp). Bake for 20 minutes, then remove from the oven and take off the top baking sheet. Lower the oven to 200°C/fan 180°C/gas mark 6.

3 Mix together the Dijon mustard and crème fraîche and set aside. On a lightly floured work surface, roll out the remaining pastry into a rectangle about 2cm larger on all sides than your base. Spread half the mustard mixture evenly over the cooked pastry base, leaving a 1cm border all round. Top with a layer of ham, then all the Gruyère and finally another layer of ham. Spread over the remaining mustard mixture. Brush the border with beaten egg.

4 Now place your uncooked pastry rectangle on top, press the edges firmly together and trim if necessary. You can make a pattern around the edges using a fork, or by crimping the pastry between your fingers and thumb (see page 210). Brush the whole thing with beaten egg and sprinkle generously with grated Parmesan.

5 Bake in the oven for 30 minutes or until puffy and golden brown. Set aside to cool for 15 minutes. Cut into 6–8 triangles and serve with a peppery green salad.

beef bourguignon pie

SERVES 6–8
*Equipment: 1 x 3-litre lidded
ovenproof casserole pan; 1 x 2-litre
ovenproof pie dish*

4 tbsp olive oil
550g lean beef, e.g. chuck, blade
   or topside, cut into 3cm chunks
200g smoked bacon lardons
300g shallots, halved
1 large garlic clove, finely chopped
500g chestnut mushrooms, halved
3–4 sprigs of fresh thyme, leaves
   stripped and roughly chopped
2 heaped tbsp plain flour, plus
   a little for dusting
1 tbsp Bovril
250ml red wine
450ml good-quality hot beef stock
700g all-butter puff pastry
1 medium egg, beaten
Polenta, for sprinkling (optional)
Freshly ground black pepper
Garlicky Green Beans, to serve
   (see page 198)

This is one of our favourite pies, with its meltingly soft pieces of beef, salty bacon lardons and rich red wine gravy. You can forget the pastry lining if you wish and just go for the crispy rough-puff lid, but we prefer it like this. It is worth making the stew a day or two ahead, as it becomes even more tasty.

1 Preheat the oven to 180°C/fan 160°C/gas mark 4. Heat 2 tablespoons of the oil in the casserole pan over a high heat. Add half the beef and cook until browned. Transfer to a large bowl, then repeat with the rest of the beef.

2 Add another tablespoon of oil to the empty pan, then add the bacon and cook over a high heat until just golden. Transfer to the bowl with the beef. You may have some lovely burnt bits left on the bottom of the pan – don't throw these away as they add flavour. Splash in some water, scrape them up with a spatula or wooden spoon and add them to the beef.

3 Heat the remaining oil in the pan, add the shallots, garlic and mushrooms, and cook for 3–4 minutes over a medium heat to get a little colour. Reduce the heat and return the meat to the pan. Add the thyme and flour and stir in well. Add the Bovril, wine and stock, stir well and bring to a very gentle simmer.

4 Cover tightly with the lid and place in the centre of the oven to cook for 2½ hours or until the meat is just tender. You want this to cook slowly, with very little visible 'action', just a murmur of bubbles on the surface. If the level of the liquid looks a little low, add some water and give it a good stir. Check on it every 40 minutes or so. To see if the meat

recipe continues ⟶

simple suppers

is tender, squidge a piece between your fingers or two spoons – it should give really easily. Season with pepper (no salt) and leave to cool.

5 Turn up the oven to 220°C/fan 200°C/gas mark 7 and place a baking sheet on the middle shelf to preheat. On a lightly floured work surface, roll out two-thirds of the pastry to about 3mm thick and use it to line your pie dish, letting the excess pastry drape over the sides. Pile in the filling. Roll out the remaining pastry to about 5mm thick, to the shape of the pie, allowing enough excess to reach just over the edges. Place on the pie and trim away any excess.

6 Press the pastry edges together with your fingers to seal, or use the back of a fork. You can also crimp the edges (see page 210). Brush with beaten egg. Make two deep incisions on opposite sides of the pie – these will act as vents for steam to escape during baking.

7 Scrunch up your pastry trimmings and roll out to about 2mm thick, then cut out some pastry leaves and use them to decorate the top of the pie. Brush with more beaten egg. If you don't have time for this, you can sprinkle the top of the pie with polenta, which gives a really pretty texture.

8 Place the pie in the oven on the preheated baking sheet. Cook for 10 minutes, then lower the heat to 200°C/fan 180°C/gas mark 6 for another 30 minutes or until the top is puffy and golden. Serve with the Garlicky Green Beans on page 198.

lemony chicken pie with quick soured cream pastry

1 quantity of Quick Soured
   Cream Pastry (see page 217)
A little plain flour, for dusting
1 medium egg, beaten
Dried oregano, for sprinkling

For the stock:
2 lemons
1 carrot, peeled
1 celery stick
A few black peppercorns
1kg boneless, skinless
   chicken thighs

For the filling:
75g unsalted butter
½ a fennel bulb, finely sliced
2 medium leeks, sliced
50g plain flour
125g semi-skimmed milk
100g frozen peas
Salt and freshly ground
   black pepper

If you are tired of the old familiar chicken recipes, try this one. Filled with lemon, fennel, leeks and a stack of herbs, it makes a fantastically fresh and wholesome lunch.

1 Make the soured cream pastry following the method on page 217 and put in the fridge to rest for 30 minutes.

2 To make the stock, remove the lemon peel with a vegetable peeler and squeeze out the juice from both lemons. Set the juice aside, and pop the peel into a large pan with the carrot, celery, peppercorns and chicken thighs. Top up with water until just covering the chicken and bring to the boil, then reduce the heat and simmer for about 20 minutes or until the chicken is cooked through.

3 Remove the chicken pieces from the pan using a slotted spoon and set aside to cool. Let the stock continue to bubble until only about 600ml remains, then strain off the vegetables and reserve the liquid.

4 Using your hands, tear the chicken into strips and set aside. Melt the butter in a large frying pan over a medium heat and fry the fennel and leeks for a few minutes until the leeks are beginning to wilt. Stir in the flour and cook for 2–3 minutes until bubbling, then stir in the reserved chicken stock and

recipe continues

the milk. Bring to simmering point and cook for a couple of minutes to thicken the sauce. Stir in the reserved chicken, the peas and reserved lemon juice. Season well with salt and pepper, then set aside to cool.

5 Remove the pastry from the fridge and set to one side while you spoon the filling mixture into your pie dish (or divide between the small ones). Preheat the oven to 200°C/fan 180°C/gas mark 6.

6 On a lightly floured surface, roll out the pastry to about 3mm thick and cut out a circle slightly larger than your dish (or six small circles for individual dishes). Brush the edges of the dish (or dishes) with beaten egg and lay the pastry on top. Using a sharp knife, trim the edges to remove any excess. Brush again with egg and sprinkle with dried oregano.

7 Bake in the oven for 50 minutes or until the filling is piping hot and the pastry is golden. If making six little pies you may need to reduce the cooking time by 10 minutes.

stuffed portabella mushrooms with puff pastry umbrellas

SERVES 6

6 large portabella mushrooms
A generous knob of butter
1 red onion, roughly chopped
1 fat garlic clove, finely chopped
1 sweet potato, peeled and
    coarsely grated (approx. 160g)
150g baby spinach
4 spring onions, finely sliced
1 heaped tbsp roughly
    chopped mint
65ml double cream
65g fresh breadcrumbs
Juice and grated zest
    of 1 small lemon
100g feta cheese, crumbled
1 medium egg, beaten
320g ready-rolled all-butter
    puff pastry
A little plain flour, for dusting
Salt and freshly ground
    black pepper

Mushrooms come in many shapes and sizes, and the portabella is one of the biggest and the best. This is a great vegetarian brunch option that meat-eaters will also love.

1 Carefully remove and roughly chop the stalks from your mushrooms. Lay the tops upside down on a baking tray ready to be filled.

2 Melt the butter in a large, heavy-based frying pan over a medium heat. Cook the red onion for a minute or so, then add the garlic, grated sweet potato and chopped mushroom stalks. Fry over a medium heat for 3 minutes, then stir in the spinach. Continue to fry for about 1 minute or until the spinach has just wilted. Remove from the heat and transfer to a bowl.

3 Once cooled slightly, stir in the spring onions, mint, cream, breadcrumbs, lemon zest and juice. Add the feta, season with salt and pepper, and give everything a good stir. Pile into your waiting mushrooms and pop them into the fridge.

4 Unroll your pastry on a lightly floured work surface and cut out rounds just a little larger than your mushrooms. Remove the mushrooms from the fridge and place a pastry lid on each one to completely cover the filling. Press down slightly to secure and brush with beaten egg. Scrunch up your pastry trimmings and roll out to about 2mm thick, then cut out decorative shapes (such as mini mushrooms) and place on top. Brush with more egg and chill for 30 minutes.

5 Preheat the oven to 200°C/fan 180°C/gas mark 6. Bake the mushrooms on the top shelf of the oven for 25 minutes or until the pastry lids are puffed and golden. Serve straight away.

party pies

salmon and wasabi stacks

MAKES 20 STACKS
Equipment: 4cm fluted pastry cutter

A little plain flour, for dusting
125g all-butter puff pastry
1 medium egg, beaten
1 tbsp sesame seeds
1 tsp wasabi paste (if you like
    it hot you can use more)
3 tbsp crème fraîche
125g smoked salmon
50g radishes (5–6 medium ones)
¼ of a cucumber
    (about a 5cm chunk)

Wasabi is a pale-green Japanese horseradish and gives a real punch to smoked salmon. Try these pretty little stacks if you want to impress guests with something delicious and unusual.

1 On a lightly floured work surface, roll out the pastry to about 3mm thick. Brush the whole piece of pastry with beaten egg and sprinkle with the sesame seeds. Stamp out 20 circles, using the pastry cutter. Place on a baking sheet lined with non-stick baking paper and chill for 30 minutes.

2 Preheat the oven to 200°C/fan 180°C/gas mark 6. Bake the pastry rounds in the oven for 12 minutes or until risen and golden brown. Set aside to cool.

3 Meanwhile, mix the wasabi and crème fraîche together and set aside. Cut the smoked salmon into 3cm pieces and thinly slice the radishes. Deseed the cucumber and, using a potato peeler, cut it into thin strips (keep the skin on, as the dark green looks pretty in the finished stacks).

4 To assemble, split the baked pastry rounds horizontally in two. Spread a little of the wasabi cream on each base, add a piece of salmon, a slice of radish and a piece of cucumber. Finish each one with a puff pastry top. Secure with cocktail sticks if you like.

mini chorizo and chilli tartlets

MAKES 30–36 MINI
TARTLETS
Equipment: 30–36 mini tartlet tins; 5cm fluted pastry cutter

125g plain flour, sifted,
  plus a little for dusting
30g Parmesan cheese, grated
50g butter, chilled and diced
2 medium eggs
1 tsp ice-cold water
75g chorizo cooking sausage,
  cut into 1cm pieces
60ml double cream
1 red chilli, deseeded
  and finely chopped
2 tbsp very finely snipped
  fresh chives
Salt and freshly ground
  black pepper

We love these tiny cheesy mouthfuls of smoky chorizo, spicy red chilli and bright green chives. They're great served with the Beetroot and Feta Baskets (see photo opposite and recipe on page 62).

1 To make the pastry, place the flour and cheese in a large bowl or a food processor, add the butter and rub in with your fingertips or pulse until the mixture resembles breadcrumbs. Beat an egg with the ice-cold water and add to the mixture. Mix in with a round-bladed knife or pulse until the crumbs just come together to form a dough, adding a little more water if needed. Gather into a ball, wrap in clingfilm and chill in the fridge for 30 minutes.

2 On a lightly floured work surface, roll out the pastry to about 2mm thick. Using the pastry cutter, stamp out 30–36 circles and line your mini tartlet tins with them. Prick the pastry cases with a fork and chill for another 30 minutes.

3 Preheat the oven to 200°C/fan 180°C/gas mark 6. Combine the remaining egg with the chorizo, cream, chilli and chives, giving everything a good mix. Season generously with salt and pepper.

4 Divide the mixture between the pastry cases. We find the easiest way is to spoon the chorizo chunks in first, then top up the little cases with the creamy egg mix.

5 Bake the tartlets in the oven for 15–20 minutes or until the pastry is golden and the filling has set. Allow to cool slightly, then remove from the tins and serve.

beetroot and feta baskets

MAKES 30 CANAPÉS
*Equipment: 1 mini muffin tray;
5cm fluted pastry cutter*

8 slices of white bread,
   crusts removed
30g butter, melted,
   plus a generous knob
A pinch of ground cumin
A pinch of ground cinnamon
250g cooked beetroot, grated
15g soft brown sugar
1 tbsp red wine vinegar
75ml apple juice
30g feta cheese, crumbled
A few sprigs of fresh thyme,
   leaves stripped

These tiny tarts are packed with flavour. The contrast of the intense purple-pink beetroot with the creamy white feta is visually stunning (see the photo on page 60), but it's the sweet and salty combo that really makes these a winner. They are easy to put together, too, because they don't require a pastry base – just simple sliced bread.

1 Preheat the oven to 200°C/fan 180°C/gas mark 6.

2 Using a rolling pin, flatten the bread slices to about 2mm thick and stamp out 5cm circles with the pastry cutter. Brush one side with melted butter and push each circle into a hole in your mini muffin tray, buttered side down. Bake in the oven for 10 minutes or until just golden.

3 Melt the knob of butter over a medium heat in a heavy-based pan. Add the spices and fry for 30 seconds, then add the grated beetroot, sugar, vinegar and apple juice and stir until everything is combined. Allow to cook for 6–8 minutes or until the liquid has dissolved and the beetroot has begun to look sticky and sweet.

4 Let the beetroot mixture cool slightly, then divide between the waiting bread baskets. Sprinkle each one with feta and a few thyme leaves.

giant tomato and parmesan twists

MAKES 10–15 TWISTS

A little plain flour, for dusting
320g ready-rolled all-butter puff pastry (or any trimmings you have saved)
1 tbsp sun-dried tomato paste
1–2 tbsp chopped fresh flat-leaf parsley
1 medium egg, beaten
20g Parmesan cheese, finely grated, plus a little more for sprinkling
Freshly ground black pepper

Tip

If using fresh pastry you can freeze the twists at the end of step 4. When you come to cook them, preheat the oven as directed, pop them straight from the freezer onto a lined baking sheet and bake for approximately 15–20 minutes.

You can make these in any size or shape – but giant twists do look impressive. They are a good way to use up leftover puff pastry for a children's treat, and there's not much that can go wrong (especially if you use ready-made puff pastry). This recipe is a posh take on cheese and tomato, but you might prefer to substitute pesto (see page 202) for the tomato paste. Warm from the oven, these are pretty hard to resist!

1 Preheat the oven to 220°C/fan 200°C/gas mark 7.

2 On a lightly floured work surface, roll out the pastry into a rectangle approximately 30cm x 35cm and 1–2mm thick. Spread the sun-dried tomato paste evenly over the pastry and sprinkle with most of the chopped parsley.

3 Enclose the filling by folding the pastry in half from the longest side, creating a smaller rectangle. Roll out the filled pastry again (don't worry if some paste oozes out, it will all correct itself in the oven) into a rectangle approximately 30cm x 35cm.

4 Brush with beaten egg, then sprinkle over the Parmesan, scatter over the remaining parsley and add a generous grinding of black pepper. Cut the rectangle widthways into strips 2–3cm wide and add another sprinkling of Parmesan. Twist each strip three or four times.

5 Place on a baking sheet lined with non-stick baking paper, and brush again with beaten egg. Bake for 8–10 minutes or until golden brown. Allow to cool slightly before removing from the baking paper.

little hot dog rolls

MAKES 24 ROLLS

450g free-range pork sausages
or sausage meat
2 tbsp roughly chopped
fresh flat-leaf parsley
1 medium egg, beaten, plus
a little more for brushing
50g fresh breadcrumbs
1–2 tbsp olive oil
3 medium onions, finely sliced
A little plain flour, for dusting
500g all-butter puff pastry
Approx. 5 tbsp tomato ketchup
Salt and freshly ground
black pepper

Tip
You can prepare these up
to the end of step 5 and then
wrap in clingfilm and freeze
for up to 6 weeks. When ready
to cook, simply allow them to
'come to' for an hour at room
temperature, then brush with
beaten egg, cut and bake for 25
minutes at the temperature
given in the recipe.

Sausage rolls have the stood the test of time in the world of party nibbles, despite being sadly devalued by mass production. Even so, cheap ones sell by the million. Try our recipe and you won't look back! The photo also shows Little Three-cheese Rolls – find the recipe overleaf.

1 Preheat the oven to 200°C/fan 180°C/gas mark 6. Using a sharp knife, cut a slit down the length of each sausage (unless using sausage meat) and gently remove and discard the skin. Place the meat in a large bowl, mix in the parsley, egg and breadcrumbs, then season with salt and pepper and set aside.

2 Heat the olive oil in a frying pan over a medium heat. Add the sliced onions and fry for 5–8 minutes or until they have softened and begun to caramelise. Set aside to cool slightly.

3 On a lightly floured work surface, roll out the pastry to a 36cm square. Cut the square into three long strips, each 12cm wide. Spread or carefully squirt a little ketchup down the centre of each strip and top with your fried onions.

4 Divide the sausage meat filling into three portions and shape each into a roll the approximate length of your pastry strips. Place a roll along the centre of each strip, on top of the onions. Brush beaten egg along either side of the filling, then fold the pastry over and seal as carefully as possible. Turn the roll over so the seal is underneath. This prevents the roll opening up while cooking.

5 Brush each long roll with beaten egg. Dip a sharp knife in some flour and cut each roll into eight bite-sized pieces, to make 24 small rolls in total.

6 Place on baking sheets lined with non-stick baking paper and bake on the top shelf of the oven for 25–30 minutes until golden. Leave to cool on a wire rack before serving.

little three-cheese rolls

MAKES 24 ROLLS

2 tsp butter

1 tbsp olive oil

2 medium onions, finely diced

2 tbsp double cream

2 tbsp Dijon mustard

4 tbsp finely chopped fresh herbs
(such as a mixture of flat-leaf
parsley and chives)

1 medium egg, beaten, plus
a little more for brushing

100g mature Cheddar cheese,
finely grated

50g Parmesan cheese, finely grated

75g Cheshire or feta cheese,
crumbled

100g fresh white breadcrumbs
(you can make from stale bread)

A little plain flour, for dusting

500g all-butter puff pastry

Black onion seeds, mustard
seeds and grated Parmesan
cheese, for sprinkling

It's the mixture of three cheeses and scattering of pretty seeds that gives these little rolls the edge (see the photo on page 65). They're perfect party food – ridiculously tasty but still very affordable, and it's easy to make a big batch in advance.

1 Preheat the oven to 200°C/fan 180°C/gas mark 6.

2 Heat the butter and oil together in a pan over a low heat. Add the onions and stir until completely coated in the buttery mixture. Lower the heat, cover with a lid and cook for about 10 minutes or until the onions are soft and golden. Turn off the heat and add the cream, mustard and herbs.

3 Mix the beaten egg, cheeses and breadcrumbs in a large bowl until evenly combined, then add the onion mixture and give it all a good stir.

4 Now follow the Little Hot Dog Rolls recipe on the previous page from step 4 onwards (omitting the ketchup for these cheesy ones), and sprinkle the rolls with onion seeds or mustard seeds before you bake them. This will help you tell the rolls apart if making both types.

jubilee chicken pie

SERVES 6

Equipment: 6 x 250ml
ovenproof dishes

2 tbsp olive oil
A knob of butter
1 large onion, sliced
1 celery stick, sliced
3 free-range skinless chicken
    breasts (about 500g),
    roughly chopped
1½ tbsp medium curry powder
1 heaped tbsp plain flour
400ml hot chicken stock
300ml soured cream
2 rounded tbsp chunky mango
    chutney
100g dried apricots, diced
2 tbsp lemon juice
25g flaked almonds, toasted
1 small bunch of fresh
    coriander, leaves chopped
375g ready-rolled all-butter
    puff pastry
A little plain flour, for dusting
1 medium egg, lightly beaten
Salt and freshly ground
    black pepper

We made this pie to commemorate the Queen's Diamond Jubilee. It's stuffed with toasted almonds, sweet apricots, tender chicken and the obligatory touch of Coronation curry powder. Topped with a puff pastry crown, it's truly fit for a queen!

1 Heat the oil and butter in a frying pan over a low heat. Add the onion and celery, cover with a lid and cook for 10 minutes, then add the chicken, increase the heat and cook for another 5 minutes.

2 Sprinkle in the curry powder and flour and cook for a couple of minutes, stirring all the time. Pour in the hot stock and bring up to a gentle simmer. Let it bubble for 1 minute, then pour into a large bowl and set aside to cool. Taste to check the seasoning, adding salt and pepper if needed.

3 Stir in the soured cream, chutney, apricots, lemon juice, almonds and coriander, then divide between your ovenproof dishes. Preheat the oven to 200°C/fan 180°C/gas mark 6.

4 Unroll the pastry on to a lightly floured surface and cut out lids just slightly larger than your pie dishes. Brush the edges of the dishes with a little beaten egg, then lay the pastry over the top and press to seal. Cut a small steam hole in the centre and brush all over with beaten egg. Scrunch up your pastry trimmings and roll out to about 2mm thick. Cut out six crown shapes and use to decorate your lids. Brush again with egg.

5 Place your pies on a baking tray and bake in the oven for 30 minutes or until piping hot and the pastry is really golden.

crispy asian salmon

SERVES 6–8

3½ tbsp soy sauce
Juice and grated zest of 2 limes
1 tsp brown sugar
1 large garlic clove, crushed
1 x 700g piece of salmon tail
   fillet, skin removed, pin-boned
   (ask your fishmonger for the
   thicker end of the tail)
120g basmati rice, rinsed
A pinch of salt
1 red chilli, deseeded and
   finely chopped
2cm piece of fresh root ginger,
   peeled and finely chopped
2 tsp sesame oil
1 small bunch of fresh
   coriander, leaves chopped
4 spring onions, finely sliced
30g shelled pistachio nuts,
   roughly chopped
8 large sheets of filo pastry
60g butter, melted
Sesame seeds, for sprinkling

Here's an Asian take on the classic salmon en croute, which is also a great party piece for impressing friends!

1 In a small bowl, mix together 2 tablespoons of soy sauce, the juice and zest of 1 lime, the brown sugar and garlic. Spoon this over the salmon in a large dish. Cover and leave to marinate in the fridge for 1 hour, turning over halfway.

2 Meanwhile, put the rice in a pan with 240ml water and a pinch of salt. Bring to the boil. Lower the heat and simmer for 5 minutes, then cover and continue to cook for another 5 minutes. Stir in the chilli, ginger, sesame oil, the juice and zest of the second lime and the remaining soy sauce. Transfer to a large bowl and allow to cool completely.

3 Stir the coriander, spring onions and pistachios into the cooled rice. Remove the salmon from the marinade and pat dry with kitchen paper. Preheat the oven to 200°C/fan 180°C/gas mark 6.

4 Working quickly, brush a piece of filo all over with melted butter. Place on a baking sheet, top with a second buttered layer of filo, then repeat with another two filo sheets, brushing as you go, to make a stack of four layers. Set aside, covered with a clean tea-towel (to prevent drying out). Do the same with your remaining four filo sheets – you'll need a second baking sheet.

5 Place the piece of salmon in the middle of one filo stack and spoon the rice mixture evenly over it. Lay the second stack of filo on top. Bring the top and bottom pastry edges together, fold up neatly and twist to seal. Brush the parcel with melted butter and sprinkle with oodles of sesame seeds.

6 Bake for 35–40 minutes or until crisp and golden and the salmon is just cooked through. Allow to rest for 20 minutes before cutting into thick slices.

steak and kidney pudding

SERVES 4–6

*Equipment: 1 x 2.5–3-litre shallow
lidded ovenproof casserole pan;
1 x 2-litre pudding basin*

600g braising beef, cut into
   3cm chunks, excess fat removed
3 tbsp plain flour, seasoned with
   1 tsp salt and 1 tsp pepper
3 tbsp olive oil or beef dripping
200g lamb's kidneys (snip
   and remove the white core),
   chopped into small pieces
1 large onion, thinly sliced
170g chestnut mushrooms,
   quartered
2 medium carrots, peeled
   and diced
300ml light ale (or replace with
   beef stock if feeding children)
2 tbsp tomato purée
500ml hot beef stock
3 tbsp Worcestershire sauce
2 bay leaves
5 sprigs of fresh thyme
Salt and freshly ground
   black pepper

For the suet pastry:
Butter, for greasing
350g self-raising flour,
   plus a little for dusting
½ tsp English mustard powder
170g shredded beef suet
Some fresh thyme leaves,
   chopped

Here we've used lamb's kidney for its mild flavour, but you can go for ox, veal or pig's kidney if you like a richer taste. Alternatively, you can use chopped field mushrooms to avoid kidneys altogether.

1 Preheat the oven to 160°C/fan 140°C/gas mark 3. Dust the beef chunks with the seasoned flour.

2 Heat a little of the oil or dripping in a large frying pan over a medium–high heat. Brown the beef in batches, then transfer into your casserole pan. Toss the kidneys in any leftover flour and quickly brown them too, then add to the casserole pan.

3 Add a splash more fat to the pan, reduce the heat and cook the onion for 5 minutes to soften, then add to the casserole pan. Finally, fry the mushrooms and carrots, and add these too.

4 Pour half the ale into the empty frying pan and let it bubble for a couple of minutes, scraping with a wooden spoon to remove any stubborn bits. Pour this over the beef mixture, then add the rest of the ingredients. Stir well and bring to a very gentle simmer. Cover tightly with the lid.

5 Cook in the centre of the oven for 2½ hours or until the meat is just tender. Check on it every 40 minutes or so. You want this to cook gently, with just a murmur of bubbles on the surface, so reduce the temperature a little if it's starting to boil. If the liquid looks low, add some extra water and stir well. Once removed from the oven, season with black pepper and leave to cool completely. Remove the herbs.

6 Grease your pudding basin generously with butter. Sift the flour, mustard powder and ½ teaspoon of salt into a large bowl. Stir in the suet and thyme, then add just enough cold water (220–240ml) to bring the pastry together. Knead gently to form a ball.

7 Remove a quarter of the pastry and set aside for the lid, then roll out the rest on a lightly floured work surface to a circle approximately 30cm in diameter (and no thinner than 5mm). Lower the circle of pastry into your pudding basin and press it into the base and sides (being careful not to tear it). Trim to 2cm below the rim of the basin.

8 Spoon the cooled filling into the lined basin and level the top. Roll out the remaining pastry to fit inside the basin as a lid, using a little water to help it stick. Press the edges together to seal well and trim the excess.

9 Butter a sheet of foil and place it over your pudding basin. Scrunch the sides to seal, then tie firmly with string and make a string handle. Place a saucer in the bottom of a deep saucepan and sit the pudding basin on top. Pour in enough boiling water from the kettle to come halfway up the sides of the basin. Bring the water to the boil, then lower the heat to a simmer, cover with a tightly fitting lid and steam for 2¾ hours (topping up with more water as needed).

10 Carefully take the pudding basin out of the pan and remove the string and foil. Allow the pudding to 'come to' for 5 minutes before inverting it on to a large, lipped serving plate. Be warned – the hot filling will run as soon as you slice into it!

little lemony lamb pies with feta mash

SERVES 6

Equipment: 1 x 2.5–3-litre shallow lidded ovenproof casserole pan; 6 x 200ml ovenproof dishes or 1 x 1.5-litre ovenproof dish

1–2 tbsp plain flour
560g lamb leg, trimmed of excess fat and gristle and cut into cubes
3 tbsp olive oil
1 large red onion, finely sliced
1 large leek, sliced
1 large garlic clove, finely chopped
200ml white wine (replace with vegetable stock for children)
600ml hot vegetable stock
1 x 400g tin of haricot beans, drained and rinsed
50g pitted black olives
2 preserved lemons, quartered
½ a small bunch of fresh oregano, leaves chopped
½ a small bunch of fresh flat-leaf parsley, leaves chopped
Salt and freshly ground black pepper

For the feta mash:
750g King Edward potatoes, peeled and chopped into large pieces
A knob of butter
A splash of milk
1 tbsp roughly chopped fresh flat-leaf parsley
125g feta cheese, crumbled

Lamb, olives and lemon are some of our favourite Higgidy ingredients. Here we've crammed them into little Greek-inspired pies, with a delicious topping of cheesy, slightly salty feta mash.

1 Tip the flour into a large bowl and generously season with salt and pepper. Give it a good mix, then add the cubed lamb and toss to coat.

2 Heat half the oil in your casserole pan over a medium–high heat and fry the lamb in batches until brown all over. Set aside. Add the remaining oil to the pan and soften the onion and leek for 5 minutes. Stir in the garlic and continue to cook for 1 minute, then pour over the wine and allow to sizzle for a couple of minutes.

3 Return the lamb to the pan and pour over the stock. Bring to the boil, then cover with the lid and turn down the heat. Simmer gently for 1½ hours or until the lamb is lovely and tender. Add the beans, olives and preserved lemons and continue to cook, uncovered, for 15 minutes. Stir in the oregano and parsley, then spoon into the six little ovenproof dishes or one large dish.

4 Preheat the oven to 200°C/fan 180°C/gas mark 6. For the feta mash, boil the potatoes in salted water until tender, drain well, then mash with the butter and milk. Add the parsley and two-thirds of the feta and give it a good stir.

5 Pile the mash on to your pies (or pie), top with the rest of the crumbled feta and bake for 20 minutes or until piping hot.

melt-in-the-middle pesto chicken

SERVES 4

4 free-range boneless,
  skinless chicken breasts
4 thin slices of Parma ham
16 sheets of filo pastry
40g butter, melted
Salt and freshly ground
  black pepper

For the pesto butter:
1 small bunch of fresh basil,
  leaves picked
25g pine nuts, toasted
1 large garlic clove, crushed
20g finely grated Parmesan cheese
100g unsalted butter, softened

This lighter twist on the chicken Kiev is packed with just as much flavour. The pesto oozes out as a lovely surprise when you break through the crispy filo.

1 First make the pesto butter. Pulse the basil leaves, pine nuts and garlic in the small bowl of a food processor until coarsely chopped (or chop by hand). Add the Parmesan and ¼ teaspoon of salt and pulse again.

2 Place the softened butter in a bowl and tip in the herby mixture. Incorporate using the back of a wooden spoon until evenly distributed. Scrape out onto a sheet of clingfilm and roll into a log shape. Flatten the log, wrap in the clingfilm and chill in the fridge until solid.

3 Preheat the oven to 200°C/fan 180°C/gas mark 6. Place each chicken breast on a board and cover with a sheet of clingfilm. Using a rolling pin, bash the breasts until at least twice their original size. Season with salt and pepper.

4 Cut the pesto butter into four pieces and place a piece in the middle of each breast, then fold over the sides and ends to make neat parcels. Turn over so that the seal is underneath and wrap each one in a slice of Parma ham.

5 Lay a sheet of filo pastry on a board and brush all over with melted butter. Lay a second sheet on top, followed by a third and a fourth, brushing as you go. Place a chicken parcel in the centre and wrap it well in the filo, trimming away any pastry if you need to. Place on a baking sheet lined with non-stick baking paper and brush all over with melted butter. Repeat with the rest of the filo and chicken.

6 Bake the filo parcels in the oven for 30 minutes or until the chicken is cooked through, covering with foil if they start to brown too much. Serve warm, with a crisp green salad.

giant roasted red pepper and mushroom en croute

SERVES 8

6 large red peppers, cut
in half and deseeded
A little plain flour, for dusting
750g all-butter puff pastry
A little vegetable oil,
for greasing
75g butter
2 medium red onions,
finely chopped
250g chestnut mushrooms,
sliced
100ml double cream
250g ricotta cheese
3 heaped tbsp freshly grated
Parmesan cheese
750g fresh spinach
1 tsp freshly grated nutmeg
1 medium egg and 1 egg yolk,
beaten
Salt and freshly ground
black pepper

Parcels are always exciting to receive – especially if they're edible! For this one we've wrapped a whole lot of delicious vegetables in pastry with a layer of creamy ricotta cheese. It's big enough to feed lots of people, and as a party piece it will certainly impress your friends.

1 Preheat the oven to 200°C/fan 180°C/gas mark 6. Roast the halved peppers in the hot oven for 35–45 minutes or until their skins have charred. Remove the skins, which should be easy to tear away from the flesh. Slice each pepper half lengthways into two strips and set aside to cool.

2 On a lightly floured work surface, roll out 250g of the pastry to a rectangle measuring 30cm x 15cm and about 5mm thick. Place on a lightly oiled baking sheet and top with a second lightly oiled baking sheet (this helps weigh down the pastry to make it lovely and crisp). Bake in the oven for 20 minutes, then take out, remove the top baking sheet and set aside.

3 Meanwhile, melt 50g of the butter in a frying pan over a medium heat and cook the onions until soft. Add the mushrooms and fry for about 7 minutes until the liquid has evaporated. Pour in the cream and allow to bubble until the mushrooms are just coated. Leave to cool, then stir in the ricotta and Parmesan. Season generously with black pepper and a little salt.

4 Melt the remaining butter in a very large saucepan over a medium heat. Add the spinach and cook until the leaves have wilted and any water has bubbled away. Drain and press out all remaining moisture: this is important as you don't want the parcel to be too wet. Roughly chop the spinach and season with salt, pepper and nutmeg.

5 To assemble, cover the cooked pastry base with half your roasted pepper strips. About 1cm in from the edge of the peppers, create a ring of chopped spinach and put the creamy mushroom mixture inside this spinach ring. Finally, top with the remaining red pepper strips. You will now have quite a high mound of vegetables.

6 Roll out the remaining pastry to a rectangle approximately 35cm x 20cm and 5mm thick. Drape this over the vegetables, tucking the edges underneath your cooked pastry base (you might need another pair of hands to help here). Brush all over with beaten egg. Scrunch up your pastry trimmings and roll out to about 2mm thick, then cut out shapes to decorate your parcel, sticking them down with beaten egg. Chill in the fridge for at least 20 minutes.

7 Preheat the oven again to 200°C/fan 180°C/gas mark 6. Brush the pastry with a little more egg and bake in the oven for 35–40 minutes or until cooked through and golden on top. Allow to cool for about 45 minutes, then cut into thick slices to serve – it will still be lovely and warm but giving it this time to rest makes it easier to cut.

wonderful wedding pie

**FOR 1 MEDIUM PIE
(MIDDLE TIER)**
*Equipment: 1 x 20cm springform
cake tin, 10cm deep*

For the hot-water crust pastry:
250g lard
1 tsp salt
750g plain flour, plus a little
   for dusting
1 egg, plus a beaten egg for glazing

For the filling:
500g lean pork shoulder,
   cut into 1cm cubes
400g sausage meat
150g smoked streaky bacon
   rashers, cut into 5mm strips
   using kitchen scissors
1 small bunch of fresh thyme,
   leaves stripped
1 tsp freshly grated nutmeg
2 tbsp redcurrant jelly
1 egg, beaten
50g fresh breadcrumbs
2 duck breasts (about 300g),
   skin removed and meat
   cut into 5mm strips
200g semi-dried apricots
Salt and freshly ground
   black pepper

Tip
If you want to make the small
or large tiers, or fancy making
the whole three-tier wonder,
turn to page 81.

**This wedding pie is surely worth getting married for!
Crammed with rich duck, pork, apricots and garden
herbs, and encased in hot-water crust pastry, it's worthy
of any big celebration. But since you don't get married
every day, the main recipe is for the medium tier only
and is equally good eaten at Christmas, with lashings
of chutney. If you do want to push the boat out and
make the whole three-tier extravaganza, you'll find
the quantities and timings over the page. For special
occasions, you can decorate your pie(s) with herbs,
flowers, ribbons or even little bunches of grapes.**

1 Start by making the pastry (hot-water crust pastry is
quite a different technique from other types, so if you've
not made it before, we suggest reading the whole method
before you begin!) Pour 300ml of water into a medium
saucepan, add the lard and salt, and slowly bring to
a simmer over a medium heat. Don't allow it to boil –
you don't want any water to evaporate.

2 When the lard has melted, remove the pan from the heat
and quickly add the flour. Using a wooden spoon, beat with
gusto until all the ingredients are amalgamated into a glossy
paste. Crack in the egg and incorporate with more aggressive
mixing. Turn out the dough on to a clean, lightly floured
work surface and knead for a minute or two until smooth.

3 Reserve a third of the dough for the lid, shape into a disc,
wrap in clingfilm and place in the fridge. On a lightly floured
work surface, shape the remaining dough into a rough circle
and place in the middle of your springform tin. Work it over
the base and up the sides of the tin with your fingers until just
peeping over the top. Put in the fridge to chill for 2 hours.

recipe continues

Tips for making 3 tiers

* If making all three tiers you will need to cook them separately. It's important to cook each pie in the centre of the oven, which allows the heat to circulate, achieving a lovely even colour.

* If you're keen to get all three tiers the same shade of golden brown, we suggest making the top tier first, then mimicking the colour on the two larger tiers by increasing the cooking time in 10-minute increments until you are satisfied.

4 Preheat the oven to 190°C/fan 170°C/gas mark 5. Put the pork, sausage meat, bacon, thyme leaves, nutmeg, redcurrant jelly, beaten egg and 1 teaspoon of salt in a large bowl and mix thoroughly.

5 Sprinkle the breadcrumbs into the pastry case and put half the pork mixture into the bottom of the pie. Top with a layer of duck. Season with salt and pepper, then add a layer of apricots. Finally, top with the remaining pork mixture.

6 On a lightly floured work surface, roll the reserved pastry into a circle about 1cm wider in diameter than the top of the pie. Brush the top edges of the pie case with beaten egg and place the pastry lid on the surface of the filling. Crimp the edges to seal (see page 210). Make a 1cm hole in the centre of the pie so that steam can escape, and decorate with any leftover pastry. Now you've finished the hard bit!

7 Place the pie on a baking tray and bake for 30 minutes, then reduce the oven temperature to 160°C/fan 140°C/ gas mark 3 and bake for a further 1½ hours or until the pastry has turned a deep golden brown. Take the pie out and allow it to cool for 15 minutes before removing from the tin.

8 To make the pie really glossy, you can brush with more beaten egg and put it back in the oven without the tin for another 20 minutes or until the pastry is lovely and golden, but this is optional if you don't have time. Before serving, allow the pie to rest overnight in the coolest room of the house. It can be kept in the fridge for up to 5 days if not required immediately (giving you time to make the other tiers if you wish).

Here are quantities for the top and bottom tiers, plus the total amounts needed for the whole three-tier pie (see also the tips opposite). For the medium-sized middle tier, see page 79.

	FOR THE SMALL (TOP) TIER	FOR THE LARGE (BOTTOM) TIER	FOR THE WHOLE WEDDING PIE!
Equipment:	1 x 15cm springform tin, 8cm deep	1 x 25cm springform tin, 10cm deep	3 x springform tins: 15cm (8cm deep), 20cm and 25cm (both 10cm deep)

For the hot-water crust pastry:

Hot water	150ml	450ml	900ml
Lard	125g	375g	750g
Salt	½ tsp	1 tsp	2½ tsp
Plain flour, plus a little for dusting	375g	1.125kg	2.25kg
Eggs	1 yolk, plus 1 beaten egg for glazing	1 egg + 1 yolk, plus 1 beaten egg for glazing	3 eggs + 1 yolk, plus 2 beaten eggs for glazing

For the filling:

Lean pork shoulder, cut into 1cm cubes	250g	750g	1.5kg
Sausage meat	200g	600g	1.2kg
Smoked streaky bacon rashers, cut into 5mm strips using kitchen scissors	75g	225g	450g
Fresh thyme, leaves stripped	Small bunch	1 x 30g bunch	Large bunch
Freshly grated nutmeg	½ tsp	1½ tsp	1 tbsp
Redcurrant jelly	1 tbsp	3 tbsp	6 tbsp
Eggs, beaten	1 yolk	1 egg + 1 yolk	2 eggs + 2 yolks
Salt	½ tsp	1½ tsp	1 tbsp
Fresh breadcrumbs	25g	75g	150g
Duck breasts, skin removed, meat cut into 5mm strips	1 (about 150g)	3 (about 550g)	6 (about 1kg)
Semi-dried apricots	100g	300g	600g

Follow method on p79–80 but use these cooking times: (see p80 for fan/gas marks)	15 mins (at 190°C), then 1 hour 20 mins (at 160°C)	30 mins (at 190°C), then 1 hour 40 mins (at 160°C)	See p80 and other columns for timings for each tier

christmas turkey pie with all the trimmings

SERVES 10

A little plain flour, for dusting
750g all-butter puff pastry
A little oil, for greasing

For the apricot stuffing:
A knob of butter
1 medium onion, finely chopped
1 tsp fresh thyme leaves
1 tsp chopped fresh flat-leaf parsley
1 tsp chopped fresh sage
50g dried breadcrumbs
50g dried apricots, roughly chopped
250g good-quality sausage meat
Salt and freshly ground black pepper

For the chestnut and bacon filling:
3 knobs of butter
1 tbsp olive oil
1 medium onion, finely chopped
1 leek, finely chopped
1 celery stick, roughly chopped
1 tsp fresh thyme leaves
250g white mushrooms,
   thickly sliced
130g pancetta lardons
100g vacuum-packed cooked
   chestnuts, roughly chopped
1 tbsp plain flour
100ml hot chicken stock
150ml single cream

To assemble and serve:
300g turkey escalopes
1 x 400g tin of apricot halves
1 medium egg, beaten
Cranberry sauce, to serve

The beloved Christmas lunch shouldn't be exclusive to 25 December. Now you can indulge at any time of year! Chestnuts, turkey, bacon and sausage meat are encased in a gorgeous golden parcel, which is great eaten hot, warm or cold, and very easy to prepare ahead.

1 Preheat the oven to 200°C/fan 180°C/gas mark 6.

2 On a lightly floured surface, roll out 250g of the pastry to a rectangle measuring 30cm x 15cm and about 3mm thick. Place on a lightly oiled baking sheet and top with a second baking sheet, also lightly oiled (this helps weigh down the pastry to make it lovely and crisp). Bake for 20 minutes, then remove from the oven and set aside.

3 To make the apricot stuffing, melt the butter in a pan over a medium heat and add the onion. Stir for a minute, then cover with a lid and cook gently for about 5 minutes or until the onion is just soft. Add the herbs, breadcrumbs and apricots and stir well. Remove from the heat and leave to cool. Once completely cold, add the sausage meat, season with salt and pepper, and mix with your hands until evenly combined.

4 For the chestnut filling, melt a knob of butter with the oil in a frying pan over a low heat. Add the onion and leek, stir well, then cover with a lid and cook for 6–7 minutes or until the vegetables are just soft. Remove to a bowl and set aside. Pop another knob of butter into the pan, increase the heat

recipe continues \searrow

and fry the celery, thyme and mushrooms for about 4 minutes or until the mushrooms are soft and golden. Add to the bowl with the vegetables.

5 Melt the remaining knob of butter in the pan and fry the pancetta lardons for 4–5 minutes or until they have just turned golden brown. Tip in the cooked vegetables and chestnuts. Stir well, then add the flour and stir again. Over a medium heat, pour in the chicken stock and bring to the boil. Allow to bubble for 1 minute, then add the cream and immediately turn off the heat. Season with pepper and set aside to cool completely.

6 When ready to assemble, cover the cooked pastry base with the stuffing, leaving a 1cm border. Bash the turkey escalopes with a rolling pin until flattish and lay them over the stuffing. Place the apricot halves face down along the middle of the turkey, then carefully spoon the chestnut and bacon filling over the top. You will have quite a high mound by now!

7 Roll your remaining pastry to a rectangle approximately 35cm x 20cm and about 3mm thick, and drape it over the filling, tucking the edges underneath your cooked pastry base (you might need another pair of hands to help you here). Brush with the beaten egg. Scrunch up the pastry trimmings and roll out to about 2mm thick. Cut out stars or holly leaves and use to decorate your parcel, sticking them down with beaten egg. Chill in the fridge for at least 20 minutes.

8 Preheat the oven to 220°C/fan 200°C/gas mark 7. Brush the parcel with a little more beaten egg and bake for 20 minutes, then turn the oven down to 190°C/fan 170°C/gas mark 5 and bake for a final 30 minutes.

9 Allow to cool for about 45 minutes before slicing; it will still be lovely and warm but will cut more easily. Serve with cranberry sauce and roasted winter vegetables.

lamb shank pie

SERVES 6–8

Equipment: 1 x 3-litre lidded ovenproof casserole pan; 1 x 2-litre ovenproof pie dish

2 tbsp vegetable oil
2 lamb shanks
    (approx. 400g each)
2 red onions, sliced
5 garlic cloves, chopped
2 tsp ground coriander
1 tsp dried chilli flakes
2 tsp ground cumin
1 tsp paprika
1 tbsp tomato purée
2 tbsp plain flour
4 large carrots, peeled
    and cut into 3cm chunks
1 x 400g tin of chickpeas,
    drained and rinsed
50g juicy raisins
500ml full-bodied red wine
    (or use lamb stock for children)
500ml hot lamb stock
1 medium egg, beaten
Salt and freshly ground
    black pepper

For the topping:
350g all-butter puff pastry
A little plain flour, for dusting
1 medium egg, lightly beaten
1 tsp black onion seeds,
    for sprinkling

Here's a warming winter pie that makes a fabulous centrepiece for the table: lamb shanks cooked slowly with red wine, spices and sweet carrots, hidden beneath a fudgy, buttery puff pastry lid. The bones act as a pie funnel, which puts them to good use and makes the finished pie look very impressive.

1 Heat the oil in your casserole pan over a high heat and add the lamb shanks. Take care to turn each shank regularly until the meat is an even golden brown. Spend a good few minutes doing this; it is worth it for the extra flavour. Remove the shanks from the pan and set aside.

2 Add the chopped onions to the empty pan and fry over a medium heat for 3–4 minutes or until they begin to soften. Stir in the garlic, coriander, chilli flakes, cumin and paprika and continue to cook for about 30 seconds, then add the tomato purée.

3 Add the flour, carrots, chickpeas and raisins, then give everything a good stir and a healthy dose of salt and pepper. Pour over the red wine and hot stock and return the lamb shanks to the casserole pan. Cover with the lid and reduce the heat to its lowest setting. Cook, stirring occasionally, for 2½–3 hours or until the lamb is falling off the bone and the liquid has reduced. Set aside to cool.

4 Spoon out the lamb shanks on to a plate and transfer the saucy vegetables to your ovenproof pie dish. Using your hands or the back of a spoon, prise the meat from

recipe continues ⟶

the lamb shanks, tear into bite-sized pieces and add to the dish. Arrange the naked bones sticking up in the centre of the dish (which will create a steam hole) and set aside to cool completely, preferably overnight in the fridge; the flavour only improves with a bit of sitting around.

5 When you are ready to bake the pie, preheat the oven to 200°C/fan 180°C/gas mark 6. Roll out your pastry on a lightly floured work surface to about 5mm thick and cut out a lid a little larger than the top of your dish. Brush the edges of the dish with beaten egg and lay the pastry on top, using a knife to make holes for the bones to peek through. Gently press the pastry on to the edges of the dish.

6 Cut leaves from the pastry trimmings and use them to decorate the top of the pie, sticking them on with beaten egg. Brush the entire pie with more beaten egg, and sprinkle with black onion seeds. Bake in the oven for 40 minutes or until the pastry is golden and the gravy is bubbling up out of the steam holes.

dauphinoise potato and onion pie

SERVES 8

Equipment: 1 x 2.5-litre ovenproof pie dish

For the pastry:
400g plain flour, sifted,
    plus a little for dusting
A generous pinch of salt
200g butter, chilled and diced,
    plus a little more for greasing
Approx. 70ml ice-cold water

For the potato filling:
600ml double cream
200ml semi-skimmed milk
2–3 garlic cloves, crushed
1kg floury potatoes, peeled
    and cut into 3–4mm slices
3 large white onions, halved
    and very thinly sliced
    into rings
100g Gruyère cheese, grated
Dried herbs such as thyme
    or oregano (optional)
1 medium egg, lightly beaten
Salt and freshly ground
    black pepper

Here we've taken the simple potato and onion pie, and combined it with one of our favourite methods of cooking potatoes, originating from the Dauphiné region of France and consisting of thinly sliced potatoes cooked slowly with milk, cream, garlic and seasoning. The result is a stunning pie which needs nothing more with it than a crunchy salad, though a platter of cold meats also sits very comfortably alongside.

1 Start by making your pastry: place the flour and salt in a large bowl or a food processor, add the butter cubes and rub in with your fingertips or pulse until the mixture resembles breadcrumbs. Mix in the ice-cold water or pour slowly into the running processor until the pastry begins to clump and come together. Tip on to a lightly floured work surface and bring together using your hands. Shape into a disc, wrap in clingfilm and chill for at least 20 minutes.

2 Meanwhile, bring your cream, milk, garlic and a generous pinch of salt to simmering point in a medium saucepan. Simmer for a minute or two, for the garlic to infuse, then remove from the heat and allow to cool completely.

3 Preheat the oven to 200°C/fan 180°C/gas mark 6 and put a baking sheet in to heat up.

4 On a lightly floured work surface, roll out your pastry to about 3mm thick. You should have more than enough to lay over the bottom and sides of your ovenproof dish. Trim around the edges. Gather up any leftover pastry, shape into a disc and set aside.

5 Layer up the sliced potato and onion rings to cover the pastry in the bottom of the dish. Season with salt and pepper, and sprinkle over a layer of Gruyère. If you like, add a scattering of dried herbs. Then continue to layer until all the potato and onion has been used. Slowly pour over the garlicky cream mixture, allowing each addition to disappear before adding more. Season again.

6 Re-roll the pastry disc until slightly larger than the top of your dish. Brush beaten egg on to the exposed edges of the pastry already in the dish and place the pastry lid on top. Press the edges to seal. Cut a little hole, 1cm in diameter, in the top. If you want, you can make little imprints around the edge to add some interest, then brush once more with egg and place the pie in the oven on the hot baking sheet.

7 Bake the pie in the oven for 20 minutes, then reduce the temperature to 180°C/fan 160°C/gas mark 4 and bake for a further 1 hour 20 minutes. Allow the pie to sit for 20 minutes or so before serving with a crunchy green salad.

Tip
If you are a fish lover you can lay smoked or peppered mackerel fillets in between the layers of potato and onion and continue with the recipe.

hot-smoked salmon gougère

SERVES 4

Equipment: 1 x shallow round or oval ovenproof pie dish, 1.5-litre capacity

For the filling and topping:
45g butter, plus a little
    extra for greasing
30g plain flour
400ml whole milk
70g mature Cheddar
    cheese, grated
1 small bunch of fresh flat-leaf
    parsley, leaves chopped
Grated zest of 1 lemon
300g hot-smoked salmon,
    skin removed, thickly flaked
10g dried breadcrumbs
1 leek

For the cheesy gougère:
70g plain flour
¼ tsp salt
A pinch of cayenne pepper
60g unsalted butter,
    chilled and diced
2 medium eggs, lightly whisked
45g mature Cheddar
    cheese, grated

Gougère is a baked cheesy choux pastry. It is quite straightforward to make but looks incredible when it arrives at the table. We can imagine nothing better than eating this for a celebration Sunday brunch with a glass of bubbly. Spoil your mum on Mother's Day!

1 First make the filling: melt the butter in a pan over a low-medium heat. When it's foaming, add the flour and mix with a wooden spoon until smooth. Cook for 1 minute. Gradually add the milk, stirring to make a smooth sauce, then bring to a simmer and cook for 1 minute. Remove from the heat, add the cheese, parsley, lemon zest and salmon, and set aside.

2 To make the cheesy gougère, sift the flour with the salt and cayenne pepper on to a sheet of non-stick baking paper. Melt the butter in a pan with 150ml water, bring to the boil, then pour in the flour using the baking paper as a funnel. Remove from the heat and beat really vigorously with a wooden spoon for a minute or until the mixture is smooth and comes away from the sides of the pan. Set aside to cool.

3 Preheat the oven to 220°C/fan 200°C/gas mark 7.

4 Gradually beat the eggs into the cooled gougère mixture, so that it becomes smooth and shiny and drops off the spoon rather reluctantly, then stir in the cheese. Grease the pie dish, then spoon in the gougère mixture around the edges, pushing it up against the sides of the dish. Don't panic if it all looks a bit messy and sticky. Leave a well in the centre of the dish.

5 Spoon your fishy filling into the well in the middle of the dish, sprinkle over the breadcrumbs and bake for 35 minutes or until the gougère is puffed up and golden.

mini beef wellies

SERVES 4

Equipment: 2 circular templates cut from thin card, one 13cm and one 17cm in diameter

15g dried porcini mushrooms
A knob of butter
1 large banana shallot, finely chopped
2 tbsp olive oil
250g chestnut mushrooms, finely chopped
A large handful of fresh flat-leaf parsley, leaves finely chopped
70g soft blue cheese, such as Saint Agur, broken into small pieces
4 beef fillet steaks (3cm thick, about 175g each)
3 sheets of ready-rolled all-butter puff pastry
A little plain flour, for dusting
2 tbsp sun-dried tomato paste
1 medium egg yolk, lightly beaten
Salt and freshly ground black pepper
Steamed asparagus and mustard, to serve

Beef Wellington is an extravagant meal but it's worth every penny. These individual ones are ideal for really special occasions.

1 Put the dried porcini mushrooms into a small bowl and cover with freshly boiled water. Set aside for 20 minutes to soften. Then drain (reserving the liquid) and finely chop.

2 Heat the butter in a pan over a low-medium heat, add the shallot and soften for 5 minutes. Add a tablespoon of olive oil and stir in the chestnut mushrooms and chopped porcini. Season, and fry for 5 minutes. Pour over the porcini soaking liquid and cook until evaporated. Spoon the mushroom mix on to a plate and leave to cool completely, then stir in the chopped parsley and blue cheese.

3 Heat the remaining olive oil in a frying pan over a high heat. When really hot, sear your steaks for 30 seconds on each side. Remove and let them cool completely.

4 Unroll your pastry on to a lightly floured surface and cut out four 13cm circles and four 17cm circles, using your templates and a sharp knife. Place a steak in the centre of each smaller circle. Brush the tops and sides with a thin layer of tomato paste and top with some of the mushroom mix. Brush the pastry edges with beaten egg, top with a larger pastry circle and seal well. Trim if needed (but leave a 1cm border) and crimp the edge (see page 210).

5 With the tip of a sharp knife, score thin curved spokes from the centre down to the sealed edges. Brush all over with beaten egg and place in the fridge for at least 30 minutes on a baking sheet lined with non-stick baking paper.

6 Preheat the oven to 220°C/fan 200°C/gas mark 7. Bake the Wellingtons for 20 minutes for medium-rare and let them rest for 5 minutes before serving. Serve with mustard and buttery steamed asparagus.

rösti-topped chicken and pancetta pie

SERVES 6-8
*Equipment: 1 large ovenproof
pie dish, approx. 2.5 litres*

1 x 1.8–2kg whole chicken
1 carrot, 2 celery sticks,
   ½ an onion, a few peppercorns,
   for making the stock
1.25kg floury potatoes (about
   5 large ones)
225g cubed pancetta
250g chestnut mushrooms,
   cut into quarters
125g butter
800g leeks, cut into fat
   rounds, 1–2cm thick
3 tbsp roughly chopped
   fresh tarragon leaves
3 tbsp plain flour
250ml double cream
Salt and freshly ground
   black pepper

Tip

You can prepare this ahead,
prior to baking. Then either
keep in the fridge for up to 24
hours or freeze immediately
once assembled then thaw
overnight before cooking.
If it has been frozen, you
may need to increase the
cooking time to 1 hour.

**This pie is well worth the effort. You will need to cook
a chicken and make some stock, but don't be put off.
It's brilliant for feeding a crowd, and appeals to children
as well as grown-ups. It also freezes well. If you are in real
hurry you can always buy a roast chicken from the hot
counter in the supermarket instead of cooking your own
and use 600ml good-quality bought chicken stock.**

1 Place the chicken and the stock ingredients into a large
saucepan. Cover with cold water and bring to the boil. Cover
with a lid and simmer for about 1 hour 20 minutes or until
the chicken legs are wobbly and the juices run clear when the
flesh is pierced with a skewer. Carefully lift the chicken out
of the pan and set aside to cool.

2 Now reduce the stock by simmering the liquid with the lid
off for about 1 hour (depending on the size of your pan and
how much water you put in at the beginning). Continue until
about 600ml of liquid remains.

3 Preheat the oven to 200°C/fan 180°C/gas mark 6. Wash
the potatoes, place on a baking sheet and bake in the oven
for about 45 minutes or until just beginning to soften but not
cooked through. Leave until cool enough to handle, then
peel away the skins and coarsely grate the flesh into a bowl.
Season with salt and pepper. Leave the oven on.

4 Meanwhile, fry the pancetta in a large frying pan over
a high heat until just crispy, then remove and set aside.

recipe continues ⟶

Fry the mushrooms in the fat left in the pan for a couple of minutes, adding a little butter if necessary. Set aside.

5 In a separate pan, melt 50g of the butter and add the leeks and tarragon. Cover with a lid and leave to soften on a low heat for about 10 minutes. Stir in the flour and cook, stirring, for 2–3 minutes, then add your 600ml of stock. Bring to the boil, stirring all the time, then reduce the heat and simmer for about 2 minutes or until the sauce has just thickened slightly. Remove from the heat and stir in the cream. Leave the sauce to cool.

6 Remove the flesh from the chicken and roughly chop, discarding the skin. Stir into the cooled sauce with the pancetta and mushrooms. Taste and season with salt and black pepper as necessary. Spoon into your ovenproof dish.

7 Place mounds of grated potato on top of the chicken mixture, then melt the remaining butter and pour over the top. Stand the dish on a baking sheet and bake in the oven for 40 minutes or until golden and piping hot.

bonfire pumpkin pie with harissa

SERVES 8

Equipment: 1 large deep-sided roasting tin, approx. 35cm x 26cm

1 quantity of Spiced Tomato
   Sauce (see page 203)
1 small pumpkin or 1 medium
   butternut squash, peeled
   and deseeded
3 large parsnips, scrubbed
   and trimmed
2 red peppers, deseeded
1 red onion, cut into wedges
2–3 tbsp harissa paste (we
   like the Belazu brand)
2 tbsp olive oil
1 small bunch of fresh
   coriander, leaves chopped
50g unsalted butter
½ tsp smoked paprika, plus
   extra for sprinkling
6 sheets of filo pastry
Salt and freshly ground
   black pepper

For the yoghurt dip:
250ml full-fat natural yoghurt
1 large garlic clove, crushed
A small bunch of fresh mint,
   leaves roughly chopped
A squeeze of lemon juice

> ### Tip
> This goes down well at a
> bonfire party with a bowl
> of warm couscous and
> a pile of sticky sausages.

My father-in-law claims he would prefer barbecues if they were held indoors, with no smoke getting in your eyes and no summer bugs nipping at your ankles! I feel rather the same way about bonfire parties and drizzle. So at Higgidy we toast the arrival of autumn with this delicious, warming pie that can be eaten at home in front of the fire – no raincoat required!

1 Preheat the oven to 200°C/fan 180°C/gas mark 6. Make the tomato sauce according to the method on page 203.

2 Meanwhile, cut the pumpkin (or squash), parsnips and peppers into 3cm chunks and put into a large bowl with the onion wedges. Add the harissa paste, olive oil and 1 teaspoon of salt and mix well. Spread evenly over your roasting tin and pop into the oven for 30 minutes.

3 Remove the roasted vegetables from the oven and stir in the spiced tomato sauce, along with the chopped coriander and 100ml of water.

4 Melt the butter with the paprika in a small pan over a medium heat. Brush a sheet of filo with the paprika butter and lay it over the roasted vegetables. Brush the remaining sheets of filo with the butter, loosely scrunch them up and place them on top of the first piece of filo. Brush any remaining butter over the top.

5 Bake in the oven for 25–30 minutes or until the filo is golden and crisp and the filling is piping hot.

6 Meanwhile, mix the yoghurt in a bowl with the garlic, mint and lemon juice. Season with salt and pepper and serve alongside the pie.

quirky quiches and tempting tarts

parmesan baskets with cobb salad

MAKES 6 BASKETS

100g Parmesan cheese, finely grated (about 15g per basket)
6 quail's eggs
6–8 rashers of pancetta
1 Little Gem lettuce and a handful of mixed salad leaves
½ a fresh red chilli, deseeded and finely chopped
2 tbsp fresh coriander leaves
Blue cheese, for sprinkling (optional)
Cracked black pepper

For the dressing:
2 tbsp extra-virgin olive oil
1 tbsp red wine vinegar
2 tsp Dijon mustard

These lacy little homemade baskets look and taste amazing and are far simpler to make than you might imagine. You can fill the baskets with any number of ingredients, but our favourite is a fresh Cobb salad with crispy pancetta and soft-boiled quail's eggs.

1 Place a non-stick crêpe or frying pan on a medium–high heat. Sprinkle a thin covering of grated Parmesan over the base in a 15cm circle. Leave for about 30 seconds or until the cheese begins to melt and almost bubble. The cheese should be pale golden in colour.

2 Remove the pan from the heat and leave to cool for about 30 seconds. As the cheese firms, push the tip of a palette knife underneath to loosen it. Ease out of the pan and drape over an upturned ramekin until the cheese solidifies. Use the remaining cheese to make five more baskets.

3 Now it's time to make the salad. First cook your beautiful quail's eggs by dropping them into gently simmering water to cook for 3 minutes. Carefully remove the eggs and run them under cold water until cool enough to handle. Gently peel off the shells and slice each egg in half.

4 Next, fry the pancetta in a non-stick frying pan over a high heat on both sides until crisp. Remove from the pan and place on kitchen paper to drain, then break into shards.

5 Put the lettuce leaves, pancetta shards, chilli and coriander leaves into a medium-sized bowl. Combine all the dressing ingredients and drizzle over the salad.

6 Divide the dressed salad between the Parmesan baskets and top with the quail's eggs, some cracked black pepper and a little scattering of blue cheese if you fancy.

wintry quiche with walnutty pastry

Equipment: 1 loose-bottomed fluted rectangular tart tin, 30cm x 20cm

For the walnut pastry:
40g walnuts
200g plain flour, plus
a little for dusting
½ tsp salt
100g unsalted butter,
chilled and diced
1 medium egg, beaten

For the filling:
90g kale, shredded
2 tbsp olive oil
1 large leek, sliced
1 red onion, finely sliced
2 garlic cloves, finely chopped
½ tsp dried chilli flakes
8 chipolata sausages
500ml double cream
2 medium eggs and
2 egg yolks, whisked
1 tbsp Dijon mustard
55g mature Cheddar cheese,
finely grated
Salt and freshly ground
black pepper

One of our staple family suppers is sausages, heaps of steaming kale cabbage and buttery mash. We thought we'd try the sausage and kale combo in a quiche – it really works!

1 For the pastry, whiz the walnuts in a food processor with 2 tablespoons of the flour until finely ground, then add the remaining flour and the salt and whiz again to mix. Now add the butter and pulse until it looks like fine breadcrumbs. Add the egg and pulse quickly until the pastry just starts to come together. Tip on to a lightly floured work surface and shape into a disc. Wrap in clingfilm and chill for 30 minutes.

2 On a lightly floured work surface, roll out the pastry to about 3mm thick and big enough to line your tin. Press the pastry carefully into the tin, making sure the edges sit just proud of the rim, and trim the excess pastry. Prick the base all over with a fork and chill for 30 minutes.

3 Preheat the oven to 200°C/fan 180°C/gas mark 6 and put a baking sheet in to heat up.

4 Remove the tart tin from the fridge, line with non-stick baking paper and fill with baking beans (see page 211). Place on the hot baking sheet in the oven and cook for 20 minutes, then remove the paper and beans, and return to the oven for a further 10 minutes. Set aside, leaving the oven switched on.

recipe continues ⟶

5 Bring a pan of salted water to the boil and blanch the kale for 2–3 minutes or until tender. Drain, then run it under cold water, drain again well and set aside.

6 Heat half the oil in a large pan over a low heat and add the leek and onion. Season with salt and pepper and cook for 10 minutes to soften. Stir in the garlic and chilli flakes and continue to cook for a couple of minutes more. Then spoon into a bowl and set aside to cool.

7 Add the remaining oil to the empty pan, set over a medium heat and cook the chipolatas until browned all over and cooked through. Remove and set aside to cool.

8 Whisk together the cream, eggs, mustard, two-thirds of the cheese and some salt and pepper. Spoon the onion, leek and kale over the base of your tart case. Top with the chipolatas and pour over the cream mix. Sprinkle over the remaining cheese. Carefully transfer to the hot baking sheet in the oven and cook for 40 minutes or until golden and set. Remove and leave to stand for 5 minutes before serving.

baby new potato, leek and goat's cheese tart

SERVES 6

Equipment: 1 x 23cm loose-bottomed round tart tin

1 quantity of Savoury
  Shortcrust Pastry
  (see page 212 or use
  ready-made pastry)
A little plain flour,
  for dusting

For the filling:
50g butter
325g leeks, stripped of
  tough outer leaves, halved
  lengthways and sliced into
  5mm crescents
2 tsp roughly chopped
  fresh sage
1 tbsp Dijon mustard
2 tbsp cider vinegar
3 medium eggs
225ml double cream
250g baby new potatoes,
  each cut in half, parboiled
125g soft goat's cheese
Salt and freshly ground
  black pepper

This lovely, chunky 'all-in-one' tart will satisfy even a hungry lad's appetite. Be bold and serve with nothing but a few salad leaves and a glass of chilled cider.

1 Make the shortcrust pastry according to the method on page 212 and put in the fridge to rest for 30 minutes before using.

2 On a lightly floured surface, roll out the pastry to about 3mm thick and line your tin with it, making sure the edge of the pastry stands a little proud above the rim. Trim the edges, prick the base with a fork and return to the fridge for 30 minutes. Don't be tempted to skip this step – it helps prevent shrinkage in the oven.

3 Preheat the oven to 200°C/fan 180°C/gas mark 6 and put a baking sheet in to heat up. Melt the butter in a large shallow pan over a low heat and add the leeks and sage..Cover and cook for about 15 minutes until soft but not coloured. Stir in the mustard, vinegar and a pinch of salt and pepper, and continue to cook for a minute or two until the liquid has evaporated.

4 Remove the tart tin from the fridge, line it with crumpled non-stick baking paper, and fill with baking beans (see page 211). Bake on the hot baking sheet for 20 minutes, then remove the paper and beans and return to the oven for a further 5 minutes. Remove and reduce the oven to 190°C/fan 170°C/gas mark 5.

5 Crack the eggs into a large bowl and gently beat in the cream until smooth. Add the mustardy leeks and parboiled potatoes and tip the whole lot into the pastry case. Top with lumps of goat's cheese and season with pepper.

6 Place back on the hot baking sheet and bake for 25 minutes, then increase the oven to 200°C/fan 180°C/gas mark 6 and bake for another 10 minutes or until the tart is a lovely golden brown. Serve hot, warm or cold.

three-onion pissaladière

This is a gutsy French classic to which we've added some sun-dried tomatoes. If you don't like anchovies, you can substitute slices of ripe goat's cheese and plenty of extra black pepper.

SERVES 6

Equipment: 1 shallow rectangular baking tray, approx. 33cm x 22cm

2 tbsp olive oil

A generous knob of butter

2 red onions, sliced

2 large white onions, sliced

6 small shallots, cut into wedges

2 large garlic cloves, finely chopped

1 small bunch of fresh thyme, leaves stripped

A little plain flour, for dusting

375g all-butter puff pastry

2 large sun-dried tomatoes in olive oil, drained and thinly sliced

Approx. 15 pitted black olives

1 x 50g tin of anchovy fillets in olive oil, drained and cut in half lengthways

1 medium egg, lightly beaten

Salt and freshly ground black pepper

1 Heat the oil and butter in a large frying pan over a low heat. Add the red and white onions and the shallots along with a good pinch of salt and pepper. Cover with a lid and cook for 20 minutes or until soft.

2 Uncover the pan, increase the heat and continue to cook for a further 10 minutes, stirring, until golden. Stir in the garlic and most of the thyme and cook for a final minute, then spoon into a bowl and set aside to cool completely.

3 Preheat the oven to 200°C/fan 180°C/gas mark 6 and put a baking sheet in to heat up. (Your cold baking tray with the pissaladière will need to sit on this to help conduct the heat and cook the pastry.)

4 On a lightly floured work surface, roll out your pastry to about 2mm thick and trim it to fit your baking tray. Score a border around the edge, about 2cm in from the sides. Spoon the golden onions over the centre of your pastry, spreading them out to the border in an even layer. Scatter with the sun-dried tomatoes and olives, then lay the anchovy fillets over the top in a lattice pattern.

5 Brush the pastry border with a little beaten egg and place the baking tray in the oven, on the hot baking sheet. Bake for 25–30 minutes or until the pastry is golden and crisp. Sprinkle with a few more fresh thyme leaves and serve.

smoked haddock frying-pan pie

SERVES 4
Equipment: 1 ovenproof lidded frying pan, approx. 18cm across base, 24cm across top

1 x 250g smoked haddock fillet, pin-boned
200ml milk
100ml double cream
40g butter, plus melted butter for brushing
1½ tbsp plain flour
1 tbsp grainy mustard
20g Parmesan cheese, finely grated
4 medium eggs, separated
1 small bunch of fresh chives, snipped
4 sheets of filo pastry
Salt and freshly ground black pepper

This is a fun tart made in a frying pan, so don't let its 'soufflé' appearance put you off! Filo pastry is simple to use and produces lots of crispy layers, which taste wonderful with the puffy golden filling.

1 Place the haddock in your ovenproof frying pan and pour over the milk and cream. Bring just to the boil, then cover with the lid, turn off the heat and leave for 10 minutes or until just cooked through. Remove the fish with a slotted spoon, peel off the skin and thickly flake the flesh. Strain the milk and cream, and set aside. Clean the pan and brush with melted butter.

2 Preheat the oven to 200°C/fan 180°C/gas mark 6 and put a baking sheet in to heat up. Heat the 40g of butter in another pan over a medium heat. Once melted, sprinkle in the flour and stir for 1 minute. Gradually pour in 200ml of the reserved milk/cream, stirring well after each addition. Bubble gently for a minute or so, to thicken. Remove and spoon into a large bowl. Stir in the mustard, Parmesan and some salt and pepper.

3 Mix the egg yolks, haddock and chives into the white sauce. In a separate bowl, whisk the egg whites until they form peaks. Add a spoonful to the haddock mixture and stir in, then very gently mix in the remaining whites.

4 Brush each sheet of filo all over with melted butter and overlap them to line the ovenproof frying pan. Scrunch the filo around the edge and brush with butter. Spoon the filling into the centre of the filo case.

5 Cook on the hob over a medium-low heat for 5 minutes, then transfer to the oven, on the hot baking sheet, and bake for 12–15 minutes or until the filling has risen and set, and the pastry is golden and crisp. Sprinkle with black pepper, then transfer to a board and cut into wedges.

cheddar ploughman tartlets

MAKES 6 TARTLETS
Equipment: 6 x 10cm fluted round tartlet tins

1 quantity of Savoury Shortcrust
   Pastry (see page 212 or use
   ready-made pastry)
A little plain flour, for dusting
1 tbsp olive oil
1 onion, finely chopped
1 medium egg and 1 egg yolk,
   whisked
200ml double cream
100g mature Cheddar cheese,
   finely grated
50g dried breadcrumbs
   (blitz a piece of toast to fine
   crumbs in the food processor)
2 tsp sun-dried tomato paste
6 tbsp tomato chutney
6 cherry tomatoes, with
   green tufts left on
Salt and freshly ground
   black pepper

Think of these tartlets as the happy lovechild of the classic ploughman's and perfect homemade pastry. They make good picnic fodder (either cold or still a little warm), or a great simple lunch with a crisp green salad.

1 Make the shortcrust pastry according to the method on page 212 and put in the fridge to rest for 30 minutes before using.

2 On a lightly floured work surface, roll out the pastry to about 2mm thick. Cut out six 15cm circles and line your tartlet tins with them. Prick the bases with a fork, then chill for 30 minutes.

3 Preheat the oven to 200°C/fan 180°C/gas mark 6 and put in a baking sheet to heat up. Heat the oil in a frying pan over a medium heat, add the onion and cook for 8 minutes to soften, then remove and set aside to cool.

4 Whisk the whole egg and egg yolk with the cream and two-thirds of the Cheddar, then season well with salt and pepper and set aside. Mix the breadcrumbs with the tomato paste and remaining cheese and set aside.

5 Place a spoonful of chutney in the middle of each tart case, spoon the onions over the top, then pour over the egg filling. Thickly sprinkle with the breadcrumbs and Cheddar mixture and finally top with a whole cherry tomato, pressing it slightly into the filling.

6 Reduce the oven to 190°C/fan 170°C/gas mark 5 and place the tartlets in the oven on the hot baking sheet. Bake for 35–40 minutes until the filling has set and the top is crispy and golden. Cool slightly, then turn out of the tins and serve with a crisp salad.

fig vol-au-vents with honeyed nuts

MAKES 4

Equipment: 1 x 10cm and
1 x 7cm round pastry cutters

For the pastry:
A little plain flour, for dusting
500g all-butter puff pastry
1 egg yolk, beaten

For the filling:
4 tbsp ricotta cheese
Grated zest of ½ a lemon
A knob of butter
70g walnuts, roughly chopped
1 tbsp runny honey,
    plus extra for drizzling
2 plump ripe figs, washed and
    each cut into 6–8 segments
2 tbsp finely chopped fresh
    mint leaves
1 tbsp finely chopped fresh
    coriander leaves
Salt and freshly ground
    black pepper

Tip

Once you have mastered these pastry cases, you can experiment with lots of different fillings: try mozzarella and fresh tomato drizzled with basil pesto (see page 202) in the summer, or blackberries with a little maple syrup and ice cream in autumn.

The thought of vol-au-vents too often conjures up dreary images of damp 1970s canapés. But no longer! These crisp hollow cases of puff pastry are filled with a wonderful mixture of creamy cheese, ripe figs and sticky nuts.

1 On a lightly floured work surface, roll out your pastry to about 3mm thick. Cut out four 10cm circles for the bases of the vol-au-vents. Then cut four further 10cm circles and remove their middles with the 7cm cutter. You will now have four hollow rings, which will be the sides of the vol-au-vents.

2 Brush the four whole pastry circles with beaten egg yolk and carefully place the hollow pastry rings on top so the sides are flush. The egg will stick the two pieces together when baking. Slide on to a lined or greased baking sheet and chill in the fridge for 30 minutes.

3 Preheat the oven to 220°C/fan 200°C/gas mark 7. Remove the baking sheet from the fridge and brush the tops of the pastry rings with more egg yolk. Reduce the oven to 200°C/fan 180°C/gas mark 6 and bake the pastry on the top shelf for 15–20 minutes or until golden. Remove from the oven and allow to cool completely.

4 In a small bowl, combine the ricotta and lemon zest. Divide the mixture between the pastry cases.

5 Put a small frying pan over a medium heat. Melt the butter until it sizzles. Throw the walnuts into the pan and coat in the warm butter. Fry for a minute or two, then add the honey. Stir to combine, then remove from the heat.

6 Add the figs, mint and coriander to the pan and season well with salt and pepper. Spoon on top of the lemony ricotta and serve, drizzled with more honey if you like.

salmon and watercress quiche with pink peppercorns

SERVES 6

Equipment: 1 loose-bottomed fluted rectangular tart tin, 30cm x 20cm

1 quantity of Savoury Shortcrust
   Pastry (see page 212 or use
   ready-made pastry)
A little plain flour, for dusting

For the filling:
3 salmon fillets (approx. 350g)
Juice of ½ a lemon
A good knob of unsalted butter
1 medium onion, finely sliced
200g new potatoes, ideally Jersey
   Royals, cut into 1.5cm chunks
   and parboiled
50g watercress (leaves picked
   and any tough stalks
   discarded), finely chopped
2 tbsp chopped fresh dill leaves
3 medium eggs, whisked
300ml double cream
½ tsp pink peppercorns,
   lightly crushed
Salt and freshly ground
   black pepper

This quiche is a nod to spring, when delicious watercress comes into season. Pastel colours make an appearance in the hedgerows and in our wardrobes, and everything looks pretty. This is a perfect recipe to serve up on an Easter table or at a sunny spring picnic.

1 Make the shortcrust pastry according to the method on page 212 and put in the fridge to rest for 30 minutes before using.

2 On a lightly floured work surface, roll out the pastry to about 3mm thick and line your tart tin with it, making sure the edge of the pastry stands just a little proud above the rim. Trim the edges, then prick the base with a fork and return it to the fridge for a further 30 minutes. Don't be tempted to skip this step – it helps prevent any shrinkage in the oven.

3 Preheat the oven to 200°C/180°C/gas mark 6 and put a baking sheet in to heat up. Tear off a sheet of foil big enough to enclose all your salmon fillets and lay it on a work surface. Put the salmon in the middle, add the lemon juice and some salt and pepper, and scrunch to seal tightly. Bake in the oven for 12 minutes, then remove and set aside to cool.

4 Take the pastry case out of the fridge, line with non-stick baking paper and fill with baking beans (see page 211). Place in the oven on the hot baking sheet and bake for 20 minutes.

recipe continues

Then remove the paper and beans and return the case to the oven for a further 5 minutes. This will allow the pastry base to dry out before you pile in the filling.

5 Reduce the oven to 180°C/160°C fan/gas mark 4. Melt the butter in a frying pan over a medium heat. Add the onion and let it soften for 8 minutes. Remove from the heat and leave to cool, then spoon evenly into the pastry case. Thickly flake the salmon (discarding the skin) and scatter it over the onions along with the parboiled potatoes and most of the chopped watercress and dill.

6 Whisk together the eggs and cream, season well with salt and pour into the pastry case. Scatter with the remaining watercress/dill and the peppercorns. Place on the hot baking sheet in the oven and bake for 30 minutes or until the filling has just set and the top is turning golden.

smoked bacon tartiflettes

Tartiflette is a French dish often served in the mountains. It is simple but rich, and the secret to making it work well is baked potatoes. Traditionally it's served with cold meats and gherkins, but we like to pair it with a simple salad of peppery leaves.

MAKES 6 TARTLETS

Equipment: 6 x 10cm deep round tartlet tins

1 quantity of Savoury Shortcrust Pastry (see page 212 or use ready-made pastry)
500g small unpeeled waxy potatoes, such as Charlotte
A little plain flour, for dusting
1 tbsp olive oil
6 rashers of streaky smoked bacon, cut into lardons
1 large onion, finely chopped
1 large garlic clove, finely chopped
50g mature Cheddar cheese, finely grated
50g Gruyère cheese, finely grated
200g crème fraîche
100g double cream
40g dried breadcrumbs (blitz a piece of toast to fine crumbs in a food processor)
Salt and freshly ground black pepper

1 Make the shortcrust pastry according to the method on page 212 and put in the fridge to rest for 30 minutes before using.

2 Preheat the oven to 200°C/fan 180°C/gas mark 6 and put a baking sheet in to heat up. Give the potatoes a wash, pop them on a baking tray and bake for 35–45 minutes, depending on size. Remove from the oven (leaving it switched on) and, when cool enough to handle, peel away the skins. Break the potatoes into rough pieces, place in a large bowl and set aside.

3 Meanwhile, on a lightly floured work surface, roll out the pastry to about 2mm thick. Cut out six 15cm circles and line your tartlet tins with them. Prick the bases with a fork and chill for 30 minutes.

4 Heat the oil in a frying pan over a medium-high heat and add the bacon. Cook for 5 minutes, then add the onion and fry for another 5 minutes or until just golden. Add the garlic and fry for a further minute. Add the contents of the frying pan to the potatoes, along with two-thirds of the cheeses, the crème fraîche and cream. Season generously with salt and pepper and mix well.

5 Heap the potato mixture into your tartlet cases. Mix the breadcrumbs with the rest of the cheese and sprinkle over. Put the tartlets into the oven on the hot baking sheet, immediately lower the temperature to 190°C/fan 170°C/gas mark 5 and bake for 35–40 minutes (covering with foil if they start to brown too much) or until the filling is piping hot and the pastry is cooked through.

roasted beetroot galette

SERVES 6

1 uncooked French golden
    beetroot, scrubbed clean
1 uncooked French candy
    beetroot, scrubbed clean
2 cooked purple beetroots
30g butter
A little plain flour, for dusting
250g all-butter puff pastry
125g mascarpone
25g hot horseradish cream
A little olive oil, for brushing
A few fresh thyme leaves
1 tbsp runny honey, warmed
Salt and freshly ground
    black pepper

This is a beautiful tart made with a little hot horseradish spread on buttery puff pastry and topped with a layer of multi-coloured beets. Beetroot has many health benefits, but one of its earliest uses was as an aphrodisiac during Roman times. Perhaps this could be a pretty starter for a Valentine's supper?

1 Start by preparing your beetroots; slice each one as thinly as you are able, 2–3mm thick. Over a low heat, melt the butter in a large frying pan and add the uncooked golden and candy beetroot slices.

2 Cut out a circle of non-stick baking paper, roughly the size of your frying pan. Scrunch it up and spread it out again into a crinkled paper circle (this helps trap steam to aid the cooking process). Lay it over your beetroot slices and allow to steam for 8 minutes or until just soft. Set aside to cool slightly.

3 Preheat the oven to 200°C/fan 180°C/gas mark 6. On a lightly floured work surface, roll out the pastry to a rectangle measuring roughly 20cm x 30cm, about 3mm thick. Transfer it to a baking sheet and score a 2cm border around the edge using a sharp knife, making sure not to cut through the pastry.

4 Place the mascarpone in a small bowl and mix to soften, then stir in the horseradish until evenly distributed. Season with a little salt and pepper. Spread the mascarpone mixture over the puff pastry, taking care not to go beyond the scored border. Top with a mixture of the softened beetroot and the ready-cooked beetroot slices. Brush each slice with olive oil, sprinkle over the thyme leaves, and bake for 30 minutes.

5 Remove from the oven and allow to cool slightly, then brush with warm honey just before serving.

our best quiche lorraine

SERVES 6
Equipment: 1 x 23cm loose-bottomed fluted round tart tin

1 quantity of Savoury Shortcrust Pastry (see page 212 or use ready-made pastry)
A little plain flour, for dusting

For the filling:
1 tbsp olive oil
125g smoked bacon lardons
1 medium onion, roughly chopped
3 garlic cloves, finely chopped
3 medium eggs
250ml double cream
125g Gruyère cheese, grated
50g thinly sliced pancetta
Salt and cracked black pepper

Tip
To make a summery version of this quiche (as shown on the front cover of the book), add 50g sun-blushed tomatoes and 50g asparagus tips (cooked briefly in boiling water) at the same time as adding the pancetta in step 7. Bake as directed and garnish with fresh parsley.

The world's most popular quiche. Enough said!

1 Make the shortcrust pastry according to the method on page 212 and put in the fridge to rest for 30 minutes before using.

2 On a lightly floured work surface, roll out the pastry to about 3mm thick and line your tart tin with it, making sure the edge of the pastry stands just a little proud above the rim. Trim the edges, then prick the base with a fork and return it to the fridge for a further 30 minutes. Don't be tempted to skip this step – it will help prevent any shrinkage in the oven.

3 Meanwhile, heat the olive oil in a frying pan over a medium heat. When hot, add the bacon lardons and fry for 3 minutes or so. Add the onion and cook for another 3 minutes, then add the garlic and cook for a further 2 minutes or until the onion is soft and the bacon has begun to crisp up. Set aside to cool slightly.

4 Preheat the oven to 200°C/fan 180°C/gas mark 6 and put a baking sheet in to heat up. Remove the pastry case from the fridge, line with non-stick baking paper and fill with baking beans (see page 210). Bake in the oven on the hot baking sheet for 20 minutes, then remove the paper and beans and return to the oven for a further 5 minutes. This will allow the base to dry out before you pile in the filling.

recipe continues

5 Reduce the oven to 180°C/160°C fan/gas mark 4. Crack the eggs into a large bowl, add the cream and grated cheese and beat gently until you have a lovely creamy mixture. Season with cracked black pepper and carefully with salt – remember that the bacon and cheese are already quite salty.

6 Sprinkle the bacon and onion mixture into the base of the pastry case (along with any lovely juices left in the pan), then gently pour over the eggy mixture. Carefully transfer to the hot baking sheet in the oven and bake for 20 minutes or until the mixture has only just begun to set.

7 Remove from the oven and, working quickly, top with the pancetta slices. Return the quiche to the oven and increase the temperature to 190°C/fan 170°C/gas mark 5. Bake for another 15 minutes or until the pancetta has just begun to turn crispy. Allow to cool for a few minutes before serving.

crispy club tartlets

MAKES 6 TARTLETS

*Equipment: 6 x 10cm deep
round fluted tartlet tins*

1 quantity of Savoury Shortcrust
    Pastry (see page 212 or use
    ready-made pastry)
A little plain flour, for dusting

For the filling:
A splash of olive oil, for frying
1 x 100g pack of thinly sliced
    smoked pancetta
4 medium eggs, lightly whisked
130g full-fat crème fraîche
40g Gruyère cheese, finely grated
1½ tbsp Dijon mustard
1 medium free-range chicken
    breast, cooked and sliced,
    skin removed
9 cherry tomatoes, halved
1 tbsp finely snipped fresh chives
Salt and freshly ground
    black pepper

**Inspired by a well-loved sandwich, we've taken the
best bits of the chicken and bacon club and crammed
them into a simple shortcrust pastry case.**

1 Make the shortcrust pastry according to the method
on page 212 and put in the fridge to rest for 30 minutes.

2 On a lightly floured work surface, roll out the pastry to
about 2mm thick. Cut out six 15cm circles and line your
tartlet tins with them. Prick the bases with a fork, then
chill for 30 minutes.

3 Preheat the oven to 200°C/fan 180°C/gas mark 6 and put
a baking sheet in to heat up. Remove the tartlet tins from
the fridge, line with crumpled non-stick baking paper and
fill with baking beans (see page 211). Bake in the oven on the
hot baking sheet for 10–15 minutes, then remove the paper
and beans and return to the oven for 5–8 minutes or until
the pastry is dry and the edges are beginning to turn golden.
Remove and reduce the oven to 190°C/fan 170°C/gas mark 5.

4 Heat the olive oil in a frying pan over a medium heat and
sizzle the pancetta on both sides for just a moment. (No more,
because it's going to be cooked again in the tartlets.) Set aside.

5 Whisk together the eggs, crème fraîche and Gruyère.
Season with a little salt and black pepper.

6 Spread the mustard over the tartlet bases, then divide the
chicken, crispy pancetta and cherry tomatoes between them,
arranging them higgledy-piggledy – it's fine if the pancetta
pokes up out of the tart cases a little. Pour over the crème
fraîche mixture and scatter with the chives. Bake in the oven
on the hot baking sheet for 15–20 minutes or until set.

lemony asparagus and ricotta tart

SERVES 8

Equipment: 1 x 23cm loose-bottomed fluted round tart tin

1 quantity of Savoury Shortcrust
  Pastry (see page 212 or use
  ready-made pastry)
A little plain flour, for dusting
1 egg yolk, beaten
Grated zest of 1 lemon,
  to serve

For the filling:
250g ricotta cheese
150g crème fraîche
50g Parmesan cheese,
  finely grated
1 small bunch of fresh dill,
  leaves chopped
Juice and grated zest of 1 lemon
200g asparagus spears, woody
  ends removed
75g podded fresh or frozen
  broad beans
Salt and freshly ground
  black pepper

For the dressing:
2 tbsp extra-virgin olive oil
A squeeze of lemon juice

This is a beautiful tart to celebrate the asparagus season. If you can't get hold of asparagus (its season is quite short), substitute griddled courgette ribbons or roasted cherry tomatoes.

1 Make the shortcrust pastry according to the method on page 212 and put in the fridge to rest for 30 minutes before using.

2 On a lightly floured surface, roll out the pastry to about 3mm thick and line your tart tin with it, making sure the edge of the pastry stands just a little proud above the rim. Trim the edges, then prick the base with a fork and return it to the fridge for a further 30 minutes. Don't be tempted to skip this step – it will help prevent shrinkage in the oven.

3 Preheat the oven to 200°C/fan 180°C/gas mark 6 and put a baking sheet in to heat up. Remove your tin from the fridge, line with non-stick baking paper and fill with baking beans (see page 211). Bake on the hot baking sheet in the oven for 20 minutes, then remove the paper and beans, brush with beaten egg yolk and bake for a further 10–15 minutes or until golden. Remove and let cool, then carefully remove the tin.

4 For the filling, beat together the ricotta and crème fraîche and stir in the Parmesan, dill, lemon zest and juice and a little salt and pepper. Bring a large pan of salted water to the boil. Cook the asparagus and broad beans for 2–3 minutes or until just tender, then drain and run under the cold tap to stop them cooking further. Squeeze the beans from their skins.

5 Once the tart case is completely cool, spoon in the creamy filling and arrange the asparagus and broad beans on top. Whisk the dressing ingredients together and brush or drizzle over the tart. Scatter with lemon zest and serve in thick slices.

courgette and taleggio tart with walnutty pastry

SERVES 6
Equipment: 1 x 23cm loose-bottomed deep round tart tin

1 quantity of Savoury Shortcrust
  Pastry with 50g walnuts added
  (see pages 212–13)
A little plain flour, for dusting

For the filling:
1 tbsp olive oil
1 red onion, finely chopped
3 large garlic cloves, finely chopped
1 medium egg and 2 egg yolks
200ml double cream
150g taleggio cheese, rind
  removed, cut into 1cm chunks
140g grated courgettes
  (about 2 smallish ones,
  weighed after grating)
Grated zest of 1 lemon
Salt and freshly ground
  black pepper

Tip
If you love walnuts, scatter
a few on top after baking for
an added nutty hit.

This tart celebrates the spring season and features taleggio, a yummy, soft, cow's milk cheese that comes from northern Italy and is now readily available in supermarkets. Like mozzarella, it gets even more delicious when melted, especially when gently oozing from this tart. If you can't find taleggio, you can use mozzarella as an alternative, though it does have a slightly milder taste.

1 Make the shortcrust pastry according to the method on pages 212–13 and put in the fridge to rest for 30 minutes.

2 On a lightly floured work surface, roll out the pastry to about 3mm thick and line your tart tin with it, making sure the edge of the pastry stands just a little proud above the rim. Trim the edges, prick the base with a fork and return to the fridge for a further 30 minutes. Don't be tempted to skip this step – it helps prevent any shrinkage in the oven.

3 Heat the olive oil in a frying pan over a medium heat and add the red onion and garlic. Fry for a few minutes or until the onion has softened and has a golden tinge. Remove from the heat and allow to cool slightly.

4 Preheat the oven to 200°C/fan 180°C/gas mark 6 and put a baking sheet in to heat up.

5 Remove the pastry case from the fridge, line with non-stick baking paper and fill with baking beans (see page 211). Place in the oven on the hot baking sheet and bake for 20 minutes, then remove the paper and beans and return the pastry case to the oven for a further 5 minutes. This will allow the base to dry out before you pile in the filling. Remove, and reduce the oven to 190°C/fan 170°C/gas mark 5.

6 Crack the whole egg into a medium-sized bowl and add the yolks. Beat lightly with a fork, then add the cream. Stir in the softened onion, three-quarters of the taleggio, three-quarters of the grated courgettes, and the lemon zest. Season with salt and pepper and pour the mixture into your waiting tart case. Top with the rest of the cheese and courgettes.

7 Place on the hot baking sheet in the oven and bake for 20 minutes, by which time the filling will be starting to set. Increase the oven to 200°C/fan 180°C/gas mark 6 and cook for a further 5 minutes, to give the top a lovely golden-brown colour. Take out of the oven and allow to cool for 10 minutes, then remove from the tin to serve.

cherry tomato tarte tatin

SERVES 6

Equipment: 1 x 23cm ovenproof non-stick frying pan or shallow fixed-base cake tin

A little plain flour, for dusting
375g all-butter puff pastry
600g cherry tomatoes (different colours, if available)
2–3 large garlic cloves, very finely chopped
2 tbsp balsamic vinegar
2 tbsp olive oil
A small handful of fresh thyme (or oregano) leaves, plus some small sprigs to garnish
Salt and freshly ground black pepper

This might look complicated, but in fact all you need are six main ingredients and a frying pan – so simple!

1 On a lightly floured work surface, roll out the pastry to about 5mm thick. Cut out a 26cm circle, place on a baking sheet and chill for at least 30 minutes.

2 Toss the tomatoes in a bowl with the garlic, balsamic vinegar, olive oil, thyme and some salt and pepper and set them aside for a minimum of 15 minutes.

3 Preheat the oven to 220°C/fan 200°C/gas mark 7 and put a baking sheet in to heat up. Spread the marinated tomatoes over the base of your frying pan or cake tin in an even layer – they should be tightly packed.

4 Drape the pastry circle over the top, tucking it in and around the sides. Place in the oven on the hot baking sheet and bake for 25–30 minutes or until the pastry is puffy, golden and crisp. Remove and set aside for no more than 3–4 minutes.

5 Place a warmed serving plate on top of the pastry and carefully invert, then give the whole thing a firm tap or shake and remove the pan. Everything should come away cleanly and it will be all steamy and hot. Leave to cool for 30 minutes, then cut into wedges. Scatter with thyme sprigs, and serve with a green salad and a wodge of fresh bread.

winter couscous filo tarts

**MAKES ABOUT 6
STARTER-SIZED TARTS**
*Equipment: 1 muffin tray,
or 6 x 10cm round tartlet tins*

3–4 sheets of filo pastry
40g unsalted butter, melted,
    plus a knob for the couscous
300g butternut squash, peeled
    and cut into 1.5cm pieces
1 red onion, cut into thin wedges
4 tbsp olive oil
1 tsp ground cumin
½ tsp smoked paprika
½ tsp dried chilli flakes
50g blanched hazelnuts,
    roughly chopped
100g couscous
½ x 400g tin of chickpeas,
    drained and rinsed
A pinch of saffron threads
200ml hot vegetable stock
Juice of 1 lemon
40g dried apricots, chopped
4 tbsp chopped fresh mint
4 tbsp chopped fresh coriander
100g feta cheese, crumbled
Salt and freshly ground
    black pepper

Tip

If you've prepared the
filo baskets and couscous
ahead, we advise very
slightly reheating them
both before assembling.
Place in a moderate oven
for about 10–12 minutes.

**We're always on the lookout for recipes that can be
prepared ahead, and this is a good example. The filo
baskets can be stored in an airtight container; the
couscous can sit happily in the fridge for several hours
and you can throw it all together just before serving.**

1 Preheat the oven to 200°C/fan 180°C/gas mark 6. Lay the
sheets of filo on top of one another and slice into quarters or
eighths, depending on the size of your tins. Brush one of the
squares with butter and lay a second square on top. Brush that
with butter and top with a third piece. You can set each piece
at a different angle to make the baskets look really pretty.
Repeat until you have enough filo stacks to line your tins.

2 Brush the tray or tins with a little butter and line each
hole/tin with a filo stack, pressing well into the base and
sides. Pop into the oven to cook for 15 minutes or until crisp
and golden. Allow to cool a little so that you can handle
them, then carefully remove from the tray or tins.

3 Place the squash and onion in a shallow baking tray. Add
2 tablespoons of olive oil, sprinkle in the spices and some salt,
and give it all a good stir to evenly coat the vegetables. Roast
in the oven for 20 minutes. Add the hazelnuts and continue
to roast for a further 5 minutes.

4 Meanwhile, put the couscous into a large bowl. Stir in the
chickpeas and add the saffron and remaining oil. Season with
salt and pepper, then pour over the hot stock. Stir, then cover
with a plate or clingfilm and set aside for 10 minutes.

5 Fluff up the couscous with a fork, then squeeze in the lemon
juice and check the seasoning. Mix in the roasted vegetables
and hazelnuts, the apricots, mint, coriander and feta. Spoon
the mixture into the pastry shells and serve warm.

smoked salmon and rocket tarts

MAKES 6 TARTS
Equipment: 6 x 10cm round fluted tartlet tins

1 quantity of Savoury Shortcrust
  Pastry (see page 212 or use
  ready-made pastry)
A little plain flour, for dusting

For the filling:
1 medium egg and 1 egg
  yolk, lightly whisked
200g crème fraîche
100ml double cream
1 tbsp hot horseradish cream
3 tbsp finely grated Gruyère cheese
130g smoked salmon
Salt and freshly ground
  black pepper

To serve:
2 tbsp extra-virgin olive oil
1 tbsp lemon juice
½ tsp Dijon mustard
70g rocket
Cracked black pepper

Tip
You can make the tarts in advance to the end of step 4 and keep in the fridge overnight. When ready to serve, warm them in the oven and pile the rocket salad on top.

These little tarts are hard to beat. You use can use smoked salmon trimmings here; topped with a handful of rocket salad, it's a classy combination.

1 Make the shortcrust pastry according to the method on page 212 and put in the fridge to rest for 30 minutes before using.

2 On a lightly floured work surface, roll out the pastry to about 2mm thick. Cut out six 15cm circles and line the tart tins with them, then prick the bases with a fork. Chill in the fridge for 30 minutes.

3 Preheat the oven to 200°C/fan 180°C/gas mark 6 and put a baking sheet in to heat up. Remove the tart tins from the fridge, line with crumpled non-stick baking paper, and fill with baking beans (see page 211). Bake in the oven on the hot baking sheet for 20 minutes, then remove the paper and beans and return to the oven for a further 5 minutes or until the base is dry and the edges are beginning to turn golden. Reduce the oven to 180°C/fan 160°C/gas mark 4.

4 Whisk the whole egg and egg yolk with the crème fraîche, double cream, horseradish and cheese. Season with a little salt and lots of black pepper. Chop the salmon into small pieces, or pulse quickly in a food processor, and stir into the egg mixture. Divide among your tart cases.

5 Place them on the hot baking sheet in the oven and bake for 30 minutes or until the filling has just set. Remove from the oven and leave to cool for 10 minutes.

6 Meanwhile, whisk together the oil, lemon juice, mustard and some salt and pepper in a large bowl. Add the rocket and gently toss to coat. Pile a handful of dressed rocket on to each tartlet, sprinkle with a little cracked black pepper and serve.

slow-roast tomato tartlets with soured cream pastry

MAKES 8 TARTLETS

Equipment: 8 x 10cm round tartlet tins

1 quantity of Quick Soured
   Cream Pastry (see page 217)
A little plain flour, for dusting
12 medium tomatoes
2 tbsp fresh herbs (such
   as thyme and oregano),
   very roughly chopped
1 tsp dried chilli flakes
3 tbsp olive oil, plus more
   for drizzling
A generous knob of butter
400g shallots, thinly sliced
80g feta cheese, crumbled
Salt and freshly ground
   black pepper
Sprigs of fresh thyme,
   to garnish

When I was a child, my mum grew tomatoes in a greenhouse at the end of our garden. The tomato plants were cared for, watered daily and even talked to! I became almost jealous of them, until the middle of the summer when I was allowed in to pick an abundance of juicy fruit. I fondly remember the smell – all gardeny – and how sweet they tasted. I've created these tartlets in honour of those nurtured tomatoes.

1 Make the soured cream pastry according to the method on page 217 and put it into the fridge to rest for 30 minutes before using.

2 On a lightly floured work surface, roll out the pastry to about 3mm thick. Cut or stamp out eight 15cm circles and line your tartlet tins with them. Prick the bases with a fork and chill for 30 minutes.

3 Preheat the oven to 160°C/fan 140°C/gas mark 3. Halve the tomatoes and place in a bowl with the herbs, chilli flakes and olive oil. Season with salt and black pepper and toss until the tomatoes are well coated. Spread the tomatoes evenly on a large baking sheet and bake in the oven for about 40 minutes or until beginning to slightly shrivel. Remove and set aside. Increase the oven to 200°C/fan 180°C/ gas mark 6 and put in a baking sheet to heat up.

4 Melt a generous knob of butter in a large pan over a low heat. Add the shallots, put a lid on the pan and cook for about 15 minutes or until very soft. Remove the lid, increase the heat and cook for about 5 minutes more or until beginning to caramelise. Set aside to cool.

5 Divide the cooled buttery shallots between the pastry cases and spread out with the back of a spoon, allowing a 1cm border at the edge. Sprinkle over the feta, then arrange three tomato halves over the top and season again with salt and black pepper.

6 Drizzle with a little olive oil, and bake on the hot baking sheet in the centre of the oven for 30 minutes or until golden. Allow to cool slightly, then carefully remove from the tartlet tins. Top with sprigs of fresh thyme.

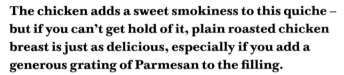

smoked chicken and parsley pesto quiche

SERVES 6

Equipment: 1 x 23cm loose-bottomed square fluted tart tin, 3cm deep

1 quantity of Savoury Shortcrust
    Pastry (see page 212 or use
    ready-made pastry)
A little plain flour, for dusting

For the filling:
2 tbsp olive oil
1 onion, finely chopped
4 spring onions, finely sliced
    (white and green parts)
200g skinless cooked smoked
    chicken breast, torn into pieces
1 small bunch of fresh flat-leaf
    parsley, leaves finely chopped
1 small bunch of fresh
    chives, snipped
Grated zest of 1 lemon
250ml double cream
3 medium eggs and 1 egg yolk,
    lightly whisked
2 tbsp roughly chopped hazelnuts
Salt and freshly ground
    black pepper
Fresh rocket leaves, to serve

The chicken adds a sweet smokiness to this quiche – but if you can't get hold of it, plain roasted chicken breast is just as delicious, especially if you add a generous grating of Parmesan to the filling.

1 Make the shortcrust pastry according to the method on page 212 and put in the fridge to rest for 30 minutes before using.

2 On a lightly floured work surface, roll out the pastry to about 3mm thick and line your tart tin with it, making sure the edge of the pastry stands just a little proud above the rim of the tin. Trim the edges, then prick the base with a fork and return it to the fridge for a further 30 minutes. Don't be tempted to skip this step – it will help prevent shrinkage in the oven.

3 Preheat the oven to 200°C/fan 180°C/gas mark 6 and put a baking sheet in to heat up. Remove the tart tin from the fridge, line with non-stick baking paper, fill with baking beans (see page 211) and bake on the hot baking sheet in the oven for 20 minutes. Remove the paper and beans and return the tart tin to the oven for 5–8 minutes or until the base has dried out.

4 Reduce the oven to 190°C/fan 170°C/gas mark 5. Heat the oil in a frying pan over a medium heat. Cook the onion for 5 minutes to soften, then stir in the spring onions and cook for another minute. Remove to a large bowl and cool. Mix in the smoked chicken, herbs and lemon zest and spoon into your cooked pastry case. Whisk the cream and eggs together and season well with salt and pepper. Pour into the pastry case and scatter the chopped hazelnuts over the top.

5 Carefully transfer to the hot baking sheet in the oven and bake for 25–30 minutes or until the filling has just set and the pastry is golden brown. Serve warm, scattered with fresh rocket leaves.

slow-cooked french onion tart

SERVES 8

Equipment: 1 x 23cm loose-bottomed round fluted tart tin

1 quantity of Savoury Shortcrust
   Pastry (see page 212 or use
   ready-made pastry)
A little plain flour, for dusting

For the filling:
1 tbsp olive oil
40g butter
4 large onions, sliced
2 tsp soft light brown sugar
A few sprigs of fresh thyme,
   leaves stripped
1 medium egg and 2 egg yolks,
   lightly whisked
300ml double cream
1 tbsp Dijon mustard
¼ tsp cayenne pepper
30g mature Cheddar cheese,
   finely grated
30g Gruyère cheese,
   finely grated
Salt and freshly ground
   black pepper

For the topping:
A knob of butter
1 medium red onion,
   sliced into rings

Some combinations just work, and cheese and onion falls neatly into that category. 'If it ain't broke, don't fix it.' So we haven't.

1 Make the shortcrust pastry according to the method on page 212 and put in the fridge to rest for 30 minutes before using.

2 On a lightly floured surface, roll out the pastry to about 3mm thick and line your tart tin with it, making sure the edge of the pastry stands just a little proud above the rim of the tin. Trim the edges, then prick the base with a fork and return it to the fridge for a further 30 minutes. Don't be tempted to skip this step – it will help prevent shrinkage in the oven.

3 Preheat the oven to 200°C/fan 180°C/gas mark 6 and put a baking sheet in to heat up.

4 Heat the oil and butter in a large pan over a low heat. Add the onions, season with salt and pepper and cover with a tightly fitting lid (or foil). Cook for 30 minutes or until the onions are soft, then remove the lid, increase the temperature and cook for 10 minutes to evaporate the liquid. Stir in the sugar and cook for 5 minutes or until the onions start to turn a light caramel colour. Remove to a bowl and set aside to cool. Add the thyme leaves.

5 Meanwhile, remove the tart tin from the fridge, line with crumpled non-stick baking paper and fill with baking beans (see page 211). Bake in the oven on the hot baking sheet for 20 minutes. Remove the paper and beans and return to the oven for a further 5 minutes to dry out the base. Remove and turn the oven down to 180°C/fan 160°C/gas mark 4.

6 Scatter the onion mixture evenly into the pastry case, then whisk the whole egg and yolks with the cream, mustard, cayenne pepper, Cheddar and half the Gruyère. Pour the egg mixture over the onions and bake in the oven on the hot baking sheet for 15 minutes.

7 For the topping, melt a knob of butter in a frying pan, add the sliced red onion and cook for a minute or so over a medium heat. Cover with a lid and reduce the heat to low. Continue to cook for 3–4 minutes or until the onion is lovely and soft.

8 Remove the tart from the oven and sprinkle the softened red onion and remaining cheese over the top. Bake for a further 15 minutes or until the pastry is golden brown and the filling has set.

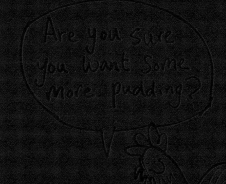

pudding pies
and sweet treats

strawberry and apricot freeform tart

SERVES 6–8

Equipment: 1 x 23–25cm pie plate or ovenproof dish, about 5cm deep

For the pastry:
250g plain flour, plus
  a little for dusting
50g icing sugar
A pinch of salt
125g very cold butter,
  cut into small cubes,
  plus extra for greasing
1 medium egg, beaten
1–2 tbsp ice-cold water
2 tbsp milk, for brushing
2 tbsp caster sugar,
  for sprinkling

For the filling:
500g strawberries, hulled
  and cut in half
500g fresh or tinned apricots,
  halved and stones removed
125g caster sugar
2 tbsp cornflour
½ tsp ground cinnamon

This is a great recipe for novice bakers and enthusiasts alike. It is foolproof, doesn't need to be perfectly neat and is a lovely way to use up slightly squidgy fruit.

1 Sift the flour, icing sugar and salt into a large bowl. Add the butter and mix with a round-bladed knife until the mixture resembles fine breadcrumbs (or pulse in a food processor). Pour in the egg and water and quickly mix in, using the knife rather than your hands, until it starts to form large clumps. Add a little more water if needed. Use your hands to bring the dough together, knead briefly on a floured surface, then form into a disc, wrap in clingfilm and chill for 30 minutes.

2 Preheat the oven to 200°C/fan 180°C/gas mark 6 and put a baking sheet on the centre shelf to heat up.

3 Lightly grease your pie plate or ovenproof dish. On a lightly floured work surface, roll out the pastry to a large circle about 3mm thick, leaving the edges ragged and uneven. Line the dish with the pastry – the edges should just drape over the sides of the dish.

4 Wash the strawberries and apricots and toss with the caster sugar, cornflour and cinnamon. Pile into the pastry-lined dish and gently bring the excess pastry up over the edges of the fruit, leaving the top open to reveal the fruit in the middle.

5 Brush the pastry edges with the milk and sprinkle with the 2 tablespoons of caster sugar. Place the dish on the hot baking sheet in the oven and bake for 45–50 minutes until golden brown and the juice is bubbling up. Serve with generous dollops of thick double cream.

sticky ginger and apple tarte tatin

SERVES 8
Equipment: 1 x 20cm fixed-based round cake tin

A little plain flour, for dusting
500g all-butter puff pastry
50g unsalted butter
100g soft dark brown sugar
3 balls of stem ginger, very
    finely chopped (approx. 40g)
2 tbsp ginger syrup (from the
    stem ginger jar)
600g Granny Smith apples,
    peeled, cored and cut
    in half (3–4 apples)
Thick double cream, to serve

Tip
This pudding can be assembled 4–6 hours in advance. Once the caramel and apples are tucked carefully under the pastry, just pop the tin in the fridge until you're ready to bake.

Tarte Tatin turns apple pie on its head! It's really not as complicated as you might think. We make ours in a cake tin rather than a pan, which we find works perfectly.

1 Preheat the oven to 220°C/fan 200°C/gas mark 7.

2 On a lightly floured work surface, roll out the pastry to about 5mm thick. Place your cake tin on top of the pastry and cut out a circle around it, allowing a 1–2cm border of excess pastry around the tin. Place your pastry circle on a baking sheet in the fridge.

3 Melt the butter in a small frying pan over a medium heat, then add the sugar and stir to break up any lumps. Add the stem ginger and ginger syrup. Shake the pan gently but do not stir, and allow to bubble for a minute. Pour this caramel into the bottom of your cake tin.

4 Arrange the apples, rounded sides facing the bottom of the tin, on top of the caramel. Squeeze in as many halves you can – any raised edges will sort themselves out in the oven. Cover with your prepared pastry circle, tucking the edges inside the tin around the apples.

5 Place in the oven and bake for 30 minutes or until the pastry is golden brown and puffed up.

6 Remove from the oven and leave to cool for 15–20 minutes, then hold a serving plate tightly over the tin and flip them both over as fast as you can. Serve warm, in slices, with thick double cream.

salted pecan fudge pie

SERVES 8

Equipment: 1 x 23cm loose-bottomed round fluted tart tin

1 quantity of Sweet Shortcrust
    Pastry (see page 215)
A little plain flour, for dusting
100g pecan nuts, chopped,
    plus 80–100g pecan halves
100g soft light brown sugar
125g butter
200ml double cream
1 tsp salt, ideally good-quality
    salt such as fleur de sel
2 medium eggs, beaten
3 tbsp apricot jam, warmed
Whipped cream or vanilla
    ice cream, to serve

This is a real classic: pastry, toasted pecans, brown sugar and cream. You can eat it cold, but it's best served straight from the oven with a large scoop of vanilla ice cream.

1 Make the sweet shortcrust pastry according to the method on page 215 and put in the fridge to rest for 30 minutes.

2 On a lightly floured work surface, roll out your pastry to about 3mm thick and line your tart tin with it, making sure the edge of the pastry stands just a little proud above the rim. Trim the edges, prick the base with a fork and return it to the fridge for a further 30 minutes. Don't be tempted to skip this step – it helps prevent any shrinkage in the oven.

3 Preheat the oven to 200°C/fan 180°C/gas mark 6 and put a baking sheet in to heat up. Remove the tin from the fridge, line with non-stick baking paper and fill with baking beans (see page 211). Bake in the oven on the hot baking sheet for 20 minutes, then remove the paper and beans and continue to cook for 5–10 minutes or until the pastry is dry. Set aside.

4 Spread the chopped pecans evenly over a baking sheet (reserve the pecan halves for later) and lightly toast in the oven for 8–10 minutes, making sure they don't burn. Set aside to cool. Reduce the oven to 180°C/fan 160°C/gas mark 4.

5 Place the sugar, butter and cream in a pan and cook over a low heat, stirring constantly, until the sugar has completely dissolved. Cool slightly, then stir in the cooled toasted nuts, salt and beaten eggs. Pour the mixture into the pastry case. Arrange the reserved pecan halves over the top of the pie in a circular pattern. Bake in the oven on the hot baking sheet for 25 minutes.

6 Take the pie out of the oven and let it cool a little, then brush the top with the warmed apricot jam. This pie is nice served just warm, with whipped cream or vanilla ice cream.

lovely lemon tart

SERVES 8

Equipment: 1 x 21cm loose-bottomed round fluted tart tin

1 quantity of Sweet Shortcrust
    Pastry, with the addition of
    the grated zest of 1 orange and
    1 lemon (see pages 215 and 213)
A little plain flour, for dusting
3 tbsp berry jam, warmed
5 medium eggs
25g butter, melted
Juice and grated zest of
    3 large unwaxed lemons
    (about 175ml juice)
150g caster sugar
Icing sugar, for dusting
Pouring cream, to serve

Tip
Don't worry if it seems like
there is too much filling.
It will sink while cooking.

It didn't take me long to learn that my husband
James has a serious 'sour' addiction: he loves grapefruit,
lime, lemon and vinegar. Anything sharp tends to be
his pudding choice, so I've perfected his favourite tart
to make him smile. Forgive me if it is a little too 'tart'
for you – it's just the way he likes it.

1 Make the sweet shortcrust pastry according to the method
on pages 215 and 213, adding the orange and lemon zest,
and put it in the fridge to rest for 30 minutes before using.

2 On a lightly floured work surface, roll out the pastry to
about 3mm thick and line your tart tin with it, making sure
the edge of the pastry stands just a little proud above the rim.
Trim the edges, prick the base with a fork and return it to
the fridge for a further 30 minutes. Don't be tempted to skip
this step – it helps prevent any shrinkage in the oven.

3 Preheat the oven to 200°C/fan 180°C/gas mark 6 and put
a baking sheet in to heat up. Remove the tin from the fridge,
line with non-stick baking paper and fill with baking beans
(see page 211). Bake on the hot baking sheet for 20 minutes,
then remove the paper and beans and return to the oven for
5 minutes or until the pastry is dry. Set aside to cool a little.

4 Reduce the oven to 150°C/fan 130°C/gas mark 2. Spread
the jam over the base of the pastry case, using the back
of the spoon to get it all nicely level.

5 In a large bowl, lightly beat the eggs, then add the melted
butter, lemon zest, juice and caster sugar. Stir well, then pour
into the jammy pastry case and bake on the hot baking sheet
for 30 minutes or until the filling has just set. Allow to cool
slightly, then remove from the tin.

6 Allow to cool completely, then add a heavy dusting of
icing sugar. Serve in thin slices, with a puddle of cream.

key lime pie with lime jelly

SERVES 8
Equipment: 1 x 23cm loose-bottomed round fluted tart tin

1 quantity of Sweet Shortcrust
    Pastry with the addition
    of 1 tbsp ground ginger
    (see pages 215 and 213)
4 medium egg yolks
1 x 400g tin of condensed milk
Juice of 4 limes (140ml) and
    grated zest of 2 limes

For the jelly:
3 sheets of gelatine
Juice of 5 limes (175ml)
    and grated zest of 1 lime
40g caster sugar
1 drop of green food colouring

For the ginger cream:
300ml double cream
2 tbsp ginger syrup (from
    a jar of stem ginger)
1 ball of stem ginger, chopped

I've spent long parts of my career living and working in Seattle. It is a city I love and where I've tasted some of the best Key lime pies (even though the recipe originally comes from the Florida Keys). The important thing for this pie is that the filling combines creamine ss with a really good citrus kick. The tangy green jelly in my version also helps to deliver that kick!

1 Make the sweet shortcrust pastry according to the method on page 214, adding the ground ginger (see page 213), and put it into the fridge to rest for 30 minutes before using.

2 Roll out the pastry to about 3mm thick and line your tart tin with it, making sure the edge of the pastry stands just a little proud above the rim. Trim the edges, prick the base with a fork and return to the fridge for 30 minutes. Don't be tempted to skip this step – it helps prevent any shrinkage in the oven.

3 Preheat the oven to 200°C/fan 180°C/gas mark 6 and put a baking sheet in to heat up. Remove your pastry case from the fridge, line with non-stick baking paper and fill with baking beans (see page 211). Bake in the oven on the

recipe continues ⟶

hot baking sheet for 20 minutes, then remove the paper and beans and return to the oven for a further 5 minutes or until the pastry is dry. Remove and set aside. Reduce the oven to 180°C/fan 160°C/gas mark 4.

4 Beat the egg yolks in a large bowl with an electric whisk for 3 minutes. Add the condensed milk and continue to whisk for a couple of minutes. Finally, whisk in the lime juice and zest. Spoon the mixture over the pastry base, swirling it with the back of a spoon to cover evenly. Bake in the oven on the hot baking sheet for 15–20 minutes or until just set. Remove and allow to cool completely, then remove from the tin and chill in the fridge.

5 For the lime jelly, soak the gelatine sheets in cold water for 5 minutes. Put the lime juice, 60ml of water and the caster sugar into a saucepan and slowly bring almost to the boil, to dissolve the sugar. Remove from the heat. Squeeze the excess water from the gelatine sheets and add them to the pan. Stir to dissolve. Add the lime zest and colouring, stir, then transfer to a jug and leave to cool for 30 minutes.

6 Pour the jelly over the top of the pie, stopping when you fear it might dribble over the sides! Return to the fridge for 1 hour to set. Combine the cream and ginger syrup in a mixing bowl and whisk to soft peaks, then stir in the chopped stem ginger and serve with slices of the finished pie.

pear and whisky tart

SERVES 6

Equipment: 1 loose-bottomed fluted rectangular tin, 36cm x 12cm x 3cm

1 quantity of Sweet Shortcrust
   Pastry (see page 215)
A little plain flour, for dusting
6 dumpy, ripe pears
3 tbsp caster sugar

For the frangipane filling:
75g butter, softened
75g light brown muscovado sugar
75g ground almonds
50g self-raising flour, sifted
2 medium eggs, beaten
Grated zest and juice of
   1 large orange

For the glaze:
2 tbsp whisky
3 tbsp marmalade, with bits

At some point during December, I find I'm through with mincemeat. This tart is perfect to pull out at those moments, when we still want a bit of warmth from our puddings. The snap of whisky and the dumpy pears sitting hugger-mugger in frangipane are just the thing to cheer up a dark winter's day.

1 Make the sweet shortcrust pastry according to the method on page 215 and put it into the fridge to rest for 30 minutes.

2 On a lightly floured work surface, roll out the pastry to about 3mm thick, then drape it over your tin, pressing it well into the sides with your fingers. Roll your rolling pin over the top to remove the excess pastry, then put the uncooked pastry case into the fridge to rest for at least 30 minutes.

3 Carefully peel the pears, removing all the skin but leaving the stalks intact. Slice off the bottoms so that the pears will sit upright on a flat surface. Heat 1 litre of water in a large saucepan, stir in the caster sugar and bring to a simmer. Gently lower the pears into the liquid and poach them for 20 minutes or until just soft. Remove with a slotted spoon and set aside to cool.

4 Meanwhile, make the frangipane filling. Using an electric whisk or a wooden spoon and a firm wrist, beat the butter,

recipe continues

sugar, ground almonds, flour, eggs and orange zest with half the orange juice until smooth and creamy.

5 Preheat the oven to 200°C/fan 180°C/gas mark 6 and put a baking sheet in to heat up. Remove your pastry base from the fridge and line up the poached pears in a row along the bottom. Using a large spoon, dollop the frangipane around the pears and gently press into the corners using the back of a smaller spoon.

6 Place the tart on the hot baking sheet in the oven and bake for 30 minutes or until the filling is just firm to the touch. Remove from the oven and set aside to cool.

7 For an elegant finish, strain the remaining orange juice into a small pan and add the whisky and marmalade. Stir over a low heat until just warm and any lumps of marmalade have melted. Using a pastry brush, dab this glaze all over the tart, allowing the liquid to seep into any cracks. That's it – serve in slices with a jug of cold cream.

orange and prune custard tart

SERVES 6

Equipment: 1 x 23cm loose-bottomed round fluted tart tin

1 quantity of Sweet Shortcrust
   Pastry (see page 215)
A little plain flour, for dusting

For the filling:
200ml fresh orange juice
250g good-quality stoneless prunes
3 medium eggs and 1 egg yolk,
   lightly whisked
50g caster sugar
450ml double cream
Grated zest of 1 orange

Tip

To check if the tart is cooked, give it a gentle shake – the surface of the custard shouldn't wobble and should be just firm to the touch.

Choose your prunes for this tart carefully. The best ones are moist, with just enough juice inside them to feel soft and not at all leathery. The fruit is poached until plump with fresh orange juice, and is then covered with a delicate custard.

1 Make the sweet shortcrust pastry according to the method on page 215 and put in the fridge to rest for 30 minutes.

2 On a lightly floured work surface, roll out the pastry to about 3mm thick and line your tart tin with it, making sure the edge of the pastry stands just a little proud above the rim. Trim the edges and prick the base with a fork. Return to the fridge for a further 30 minutes. Don't be tempted to skip this step – it helps prevent any shrinkage in the oven.

3 While the pastry is resting, place the orange juice and prunes in a small saucepan and bring to a gentle simmer. Over a low heat, allow to gently bubble for about 20 minutes or until all the liquid has evaporated. Set aside to cool.

4 Preheat the oven to 200°C/fan 180°C/gas mark 6 and put a baking sheet in to heat up. Remove the tin from the fridge, line with non-stick baking paper and fill with baking beans (see page 211). Bake in the oven on the hot baking sheet for 20 minutes, then remove the paper and beans and return to the oven for a further 5–8 minutes or until the pastry is dry. Set aside.

5 Reduce the oven temperature to 160°C/fan 140°C/ gas mark 3. Place the eggs, egg yolk, caster sugar, cream and orange zest in a large bowl and whisk together until evenly mixed. Spread the orangey prunes over the pastry base and pour over the custard. Place your tart tin in the oven on the hot baking sheet and bake for 35–40 minutes or until the custard is set. Allow to cool completely before serving.

mincemeat and apple christmas croustade

SERVES 8

200g plain flour, sifted, plus
    a little for dusting
A pinch of salt
125g butter, chilled and diced,
    plus a little melted butter
    for brushing
3 tbsp caster sugar
1 medium egg, lightly beaten,
    plus extra for brushing
30g ground almonds
2 small Bramley apples
    or 1 large one, peeled,
    cored and cut into chunks
2 small Cox's apples, cored
    and finely sliced
Brandy cream or brandy
    butter, to serve

For the mincemeat (makes 550g):
1 Bramley apple, peeled,
    cored and coarsely grated
Juice and grated zest of 1 orange
Juice and grated zest of 1 lemon
70g dried cranberries
30g flaked almonds
200g sultanas
40g suet
100g soft light brown sugar
2 tsp mixed spice
1 tbsp brandy (optional)

Tip
You can make the
mincemeat in advance
(up to 3 months) and
store in a sealed jar
in the fridge.

Think of this recipe as a giant mince pie to be shared!
We've made our own mincemeat, loaded with citrusy
zest and juice, but you can replace with 550g of shop-
bought mincemeat, which can be almost as good.

1 A few hours or a day before you want to make the
croustade, mix all the mincemeat ingredients together
and set aside, covered, to allow the flavours to develop.

2 To make the pastry, mix the flour and salt in a large bowl, or
pulse in a food processor for a couple of seconds, then add the
butter and rub in with your fingertips or pulse until you have
fine crumbs. Mix in 2 tablespoons of sugar, then add the egg
and mix with a round-bladed knife or pulse until the mixture
just starts to form large clumps. Tip on to a lightly floured
work surface and knead briefly with your hands. Shape into
a flat disc, wrap in clingfilm and chill for 30 minutes.

3 Preheat the oven to 200°C/fan 180°C/gas mark 6. Line
a baking sheet with non-stick baking paper. On a lightly
floured work surface, roll out the pastry to a 36cm circle,
about 3mm thick. Sprinkle with the ground almonds,
then transfer to the lined baking sheet.

4 Mix the Bramley apple chunks with the mincemeat
and spoon into the middle of the waiting pastry. Arrange
the Cox's apple slices in an overlapping circle in the centre,
and bring up the sides of the pastry to enclose the filling,
leaving the apple slices exposed.

5 Brush the pastry with beaten egg and the apple slices
with melted butter. Sprinkle both with the remaining caster
sugar. Bake for 40–45 minutes or until the pastry is crisp
and the filling is cooked and tender. Serve hot with brandy
cream or brandy butter.

jumble berry tart

SERVES 8

Equipment: 1 x 23cm loose-bottomed round fluted tart tin

1 quantity of Sweet Shortcrust
  Pastry (see page 215)
A little plain flour, for dusting
75g butter, softened
75g caster sugar
75g ground almonds
50g self-raising flour
2 medium eggs, beaten
Juice and grated zest
  of 1 large orange
4 tbsp berry jam,
  e.g. raspberry or woodland
200g frozen berries,
  e.g. blackberries, blueberries,
  raspberries, strawberries,
  redcurrants
15g almonds, cut into slivers
  (ones with skins look prettiest)
2 tbsp apricot jam, warmed
Thick double cream or
  crème fraîche, to serve

This gorgeous tart is full of oozy jam, sharp berries and fudgy almonds, all jumbled on top of delicious crisp pastry. It's perfect for just about any day of the year.

1 Make the sweet shortcrust pastry according to the method on page 215 and put it into the fridge to rest for 30 minutes.

2 On a lightly floured work surface, roll out your pastry to about 3mm thick, then drape it over your tart tin, pressing it well into the sides with your fingers. Roll your rolling pin over the top to remove the excess pastry. Chill the lined tart case for at least 30 minutes.

3 Meanwhile, make the frangipane for the filling. Using an electric whisk or a wooden spoon and a firm wrist, beat the butter, sugar, almonds, flour, eggs and orange juice and zest until smooth and creamy.

4 Preheat the oven to 200°C/180°C/gas mark 6 and put a baking sheet in to heat up. Remove the tart tin from the fridge and spread 2 tablespoons of jam over the pastry base. Using a large spoon, dollop the frangipane on top of the jam, spreading it evenly across the base. Toss the frozen berries in the remaining jam and sprinkle over the frangipane. Sprinkle with the slivered almonds.

5 Place the tart on the hot baking sheet in the oven and bake for 30 minutes or until the filling is just firm to the touch. If it needs a few minutes longer, reduce the oven temperature to 180°C/fan 160°C/gas mark 4. Remove the tart from the oven and set aside to cool for 30 minutes.

6 Brush the warm apricot jam all over the tart and serve warm or cold, cut into wedges, with dollops of thick double cream or crème fraîche.

honeyed nut and custard tart

SERVES 8

Equipment: 1 x 23cm loose-bottomed round fluted tart tin

For the pastry:
185g plain flour, plus
    a little for dusting
55g icing sugar
30g ground almonds
A pinch of salt
125g butter, chilled and cubed
1 egg yolk, beaten
1 tbsp ice-cold water

For the honey custard:
200ml double cream
2 eggs, lightly whisked
100g caster sugar
2 tbsp runny honey
1 tsp vanilla extract

For the nut topping:
2 tbsp runny honey, plus more
    for brushing if you like
A knob or two of butter
50g shelled pistachios,
    roughly chopped
50 walnuts, roughly chopped
50g hazelnuts, toasted
    and roughly chopped

The generous scattering of honeyed nuts on this tart is inspired by Greek baklava and sandy beaches in the sun.

1 Start by making the pastry. Sift the flour, icing sugar, ground almonds and salt into a large bowl. Rub the butter into the mixture with your fingertips until it resembles breadcrumbs (or pulse in a food processor).

2 Add the beaten egg yolk and just enough of the water to bring the mixture together, mixing with a round-bladed knife. Knead very briefly with your hands, then shape into a disc, wrap in clingfilm and chill in the fridge for 30 minutes.

3 On a lightly floured work surface, roll out the pastry to about 3mm thick and line your tart tin with it, making sure the edge of the pastry stands just a little proud above the rim. Trim the edges, prick the base with a fork and return it to the fridge for a further 30 minutes. Don't be tempted to skip this step – it helps prevent any shrinkage in the oven.

4 Preheat the oven to 200°C/fan 180°C/gas mark 6 and put a baking sheet in to heat up. Take your pastry case from the fridge, line with non-stick baking paper and fill with baking

recipe continues

beans (see page 211). Place on the hot baking sheet in the oven and bake for 20 minutes, then remove the paper and beans and return to the oven for a further 5 minutes. Remove from the oven and set aside.

5 Reduce the oven to 180°C/fan 160°C/gas mark 4. Leave the hot baking sheet inside.

6 To make the honey custard, heat the cream in a saucepan over a medium heat and bring almost to the boil. In a separate bowl, mix together the eggs, sugar, honey and vanilla extract until amalgamated. Slowly pour in the hot cream and stir well until incorporated. Try not to beat any air into the mixture – you want it to be as smooth as possible.

7 Gently pour the custard into the cooled tart case and bake on the hot baking sheet in the oven for 30 minutes or until the custard is set but not coloured. Remove from the oven.

8 The nut topping is very quick to prepare and makes the tart look fabulous. Heat the honey and a knob of butter in a small frying pan over a high heat. Throw in the nuts and coat in the buttery honey. Heat for a further 2 minutes, then tip out onto your tart and serve. Drizzle or brush with more melted butter and honey if you like it sweet.

oaty treacle tart

SERVES 8

Equipment: 1 x 23cm loose-bottomed square tart tin

1 quantity of Sweet Shortcrust
    Pastry (see page 215)
A little plain flour, for dusting

For the filling:
300g golden syrup
220ml double cream
2 medium eggs, lightly whisked
100g rolled oats
Finely grated zest of 1 lemon

Amy, who does the marketing at Higgidy, says this is the best treacle tart she's ever eaten: 'all fudgy, with a little lemony kick'.

1 Make the sweet shortcrust pastry according to the method on page 215 and put it into the fridge to rest for 30 minutes.

2 On a lightly floured work surface, roll out your pastry to about 3mm thick and line your tart tin with it, making sure the edge of the pastry stands just a little proud above the rim. Trim the edges, prick the base with a fork and return it to the fridge for a further 30 minutes. Don't be tempted to skip this step – it helps prevent any shrinkage in the oven.

3 Preheat the oven to 200°C/fan 180°C/gas mark 6 and put a baking sheet in to heat up. Remove your pastry case from the fridge, line with non-stick baking paper and fill with baking beans (see page 211). Bake in the oven on the baking sheet for 20 minutes, then remove the paper and beans and return to the oven for a further 5 minutes or until the pastry is dry. Remove and set aside. Reduce the oven to 180°C/fan 160°C/gas mark 4.

4 Warm the golden syrup in a pan over a gentle heat until tiny bubbles appear, then remove from the heat. In a medium bowl, mix the cream and eggs. Add the oats and lemon zest, and stir to combine. Lastly, pour in the warm syrup and give the whole lot a good stir with a wooden spoon. Pour into the baked pastry case.

5 Bake the tart on the ht baking sheet in the oven for about 30 minutes or until the pastry is crisp and golden and the filling feels set in the middle when gently pressed. Cool in the tin for 10–15 minutes, then remove from the tin and serve just a little bit warm.

chocolate snowflake tart

SERVES 8–10

Equipment: 1 x 23cm loose-bottomed round fluted tart tin; snowflake stencil (see intro, right)

1 quantity of Chocolate
   Shortcrust Pastry (see page 215)
A little plain flour, for dusting
300ml double cream
300g light muscovado sugar
300g dark chocolate, (at least 70% cocoa solids), broken into pieces
Icing sugar, for decorating

However organised I try to be in the run-up to Christmas, I always feel on the back foot. But this is a brilliant prepare-ahead pudding that can be made and stuck in the freezer. Leave to thaw overnight and simply decorate on the day. Snowflake stencils are available online or you can make your own by cutting snowflake shapes out of a sheet of paper. Alternatively, simply pop a sprig of holly on top.

1 Make the chocolate shortcrust pastry according to the method on page 215 and put it into the fridge to rest for 30 minutes before using.

2 On a lightly floured work surface, roll out the pastry to about 3mm thick and line the tart tin with it. Trim the edges, prick the base with a fork and chill for a further 30 minutes.

3 Preheat the oven to 200°C/fan 180°C/gas mark 6 and put a baking sheet in to heat up. Remove the tin from the fridge, line with non-stick baking paper and fill with baking beans (see page 211). Place in the oven on the hot baking sheet and bake for 20 minutes, then remove the paper and beans and return to the oven for 8–10 minutes or until dry and cooked through. Remove from the tin and leave to cool completely.

4 To make the filling, put the cream and muscovado sugar into a saucepan and heat gently until the sugar has dissolved. Add the chocolate and continue to stir over a low heat until it has melted and the mixture is beautifully smooth. Pour the filling into the cooled pastry case and leave to set in the fridge for at least 2 hours.

5 Rest your snowflake stencil on top of your tart. Using a light hand, gently sprinkle icing sugar over the top, then remove your stencil to unveil the decorations. Serve with festive cheer!

chocolate brownie puddle pie

SERVES 8

Equipment: 1 x 23cm loose-bottomed round fluted tart tin

1 quantity of Sweet Shortcrust
  Pastry (see page 215)
A little plain flour, for dusting
200g dark chocolate (at least
  70% cocoa solids), broken up
150g butter, cut into cubes,
  plus extra for greasing
2 medium eggs and 2 egg yolks
125g golden caster sugar
25g plain flour
25g cocoa powder, plus
  extra for dusting
Crème fraîche, to serve

There's something about brownies that people can't resist; somehow the fudgy, chocolaty, gooey goodness makes us forget the calorie content and have 'just a little one'. Here we've fulfilled our brownie dreams by putting them into a pie – surely nothing could be better than that?

1 Make the sweet shortcrust pastry according to the method on page 215 and put in the fridge to rest for 30 minutes.

2 On a lightly floured work surface, roll out the pastry to about 3mm thick and line your tart tin with it, making sure the edge of the pastry stands just a little proud above the rim. Trim the edges, prick the base with a fork and return it to the fridge for a further 30 minutes. Don't be tempted to skip this step – it helps prevent any shrinkage in the oven.

3 Preheat the oven to 200°C/fan 180°C/gas mark 6 and put a baking sheet in to heat up. Remove the tin from the fridge, line with non-stick baking paper and fill with baking beans (see page 211). Bake on the hot baking sheet in the oven for 20 minutes, then remove the paper and beans and return to the oven for 5 minutes or until the pastry is dry. Remove and set aside. Reduce the oven to 180°C/fan 160°C/gas mark 4.

4 To make the filling, melt the chocolate and butter in a heatproof bowl over a pan of simmering water, stirring occasionally till smooth. Set aside to cool. Using an electric whisk, beat the eggs, yolks and sugar in a separate bowl for 5 minutes or until thick and foamy. Whisk in the cooled chocolate mixture, then sift in the flour and cocoa powder and gently stir in.

5 Pour the mixture into the case and bake for 14–16 minutes or until the edges are set but the centre is still gooey. Let it sit for 5 minutes, then dust with cocoa powder and serve in slices with crème fraîche.

rhubarb crumble tarts

MAKES 6 TARTS
Equipment: 6 x 10cm round fluted tartlet tins

1 quantity of Sweet Shortcrust
　Pastry (see page 215)
A little plain flour, for dusting
600g rhubarb (the pinker the
　better!), cut into 2.5 cm pieces
120g caster sugar
Juice and grated zest
　of ½ an orange

For the crumble:
25g plain flour
30g soft light brown sugar
25g rolled oats
35g butter, chilled and diced

For the filling:
120g mascarpone
2 tbsp icing sugar
200ml double cream
½ tsp vanilla bean paste

Rhubarb crumble is a classic for good reason! Sharp rhubarb contrasts perfectly in taste and texture with sweet crumble. Here we have combined them into little tarts that are bound to impress your guests.

1 Make the sweet shortcrust pastry according to the method on page 215 and put it in the fridge to rest for 30 minutes.

2 On a lightly floured work surface, roll out the pastry to about 2mm thick. Cut out six 15cm circles, line the tins with them and prick the bases with a fork. Chill for 30 minutes.

3 Preheat the oven to 200°C/fan 180°C/gas mark 6 and put a baking sheet in to heat up. Line each tartlet case with non-stick baking paper and fill with baking beans (see page 211). Bake on the hot baking sheet in the oven for 15 minutes, then remove the paper and beans and continue to cook for 5–10 minutes or until the pastry is dry. Cool and remove from the tins. Reduce the oven to 180°C/fan 160°C/gas mark 4.

4 Toss the rhubarb in a bowl with the sugar, orange zest and juice. Spread over a shallow baking tray and bake for 20 minutes or until tender. Tip into a bowl and allow to cool.

5 For the crumble, mix the flour, sugar and oats in a bowl. Rub the butter in with your fingertips until you have coarse crumbs. Scatter over a baking sheet lined with non-stick baking paper and bake for 18–20 minutes or until golden. Break up with a wooden spoon if needed. Set aside to cool.

6 To make the filling, whip the mascarpone to loosen it, then add the sugar, cream and vanilla paste and whip until smooth. Divide between your tartlet cases, smoothing with the back of a spoon. Add the rhubarb and finish with the crumble topping. Drizzle over a little rhubarb juice to serve.

apple and blackberry pie

SERVES 8

Equipment: 1 x 18–20cm round ovenproof pie dish; pie funnel (optional)

For the pastry:
250g plain flour, plus
 a little for dusting
A pinch of salt
½ tsp ground cinnamon
250g butter, chilled and diced
2–3 tbsp ice-cold water
1 medium egg, lightly beaten

For the filling:
600g Bramley apples, peeled,
 cored and roughly chopped
 (about 6 medium apples)
1 tbsp lemon juice
40g soft light brown sugar
2 tbsp cornflour
150g fresh blackberries

For the topping:
¼ tsp ground cinnamon
1 tbsp golden caster sugar

Surely it's no coincidence that these two beautiful fruits ripen at the same time? When September comes around, my children Kate and Jack like to go blackberry picking in the lane that runs behind our house. They trot off with bowls in hand and come back with stained fingers (and often school uniforms!). Sometimes I let them don a little apron each and help me make the pastry. If you choose to follow suit, be prepared to have a flour-dusted kitchen.

1 Sift the flour, salt and cinnamon into a large bowl and stir. Add the butter and mix with a round-bladed knife until the mixture resembles small breadcrumbs (or pulse in a food processor). Add the water and quickly mix in, using the knife rather than your hands, until it starts to form large clumps (add a little more water if needed). Now use your hands to bring the dough together, then knead briefly and form into a disc. Wrap in clingfilm and chill for 30 minutes.

2 On a lightly floured work surface, roll out the pastry to a large rectangle (approx. 40cm x 25cm). With the shorter side towards you, fold the top third down to the centre and the bottom third up. Then fold in half to create a neat, square parcel. Give the pastry a quarter turn. Roll out once again to a large rectangle and repeat the folding. Wrap in clingfilm and chill again for at least 30 minutes. Overnight is best.

recipe continues ⟶

3 Preheat the oven to 200°C/fan 180°C/gas mark 6. On a lightly floured work surface, roll out the pastry to about 3mm thick. Use just more than half of it to line your pie dish, and brush with beaten egg. Use the remaining pastry to create a lid: roll a circle about 5cm wider than the diameter of your pie dish and set aside.

4 In a large bowl, gently toss the apple chunks with the lemon juice, brown sugar, cornflour and blackberries. Pile the fruit into your pastry-lined pie dish, heaping it up in the middle. Add a pie funnel, if using. Gently cover with the prepared pastry lid, cutting a funnel hole if needed. Press (don't stretch) the pastry against the fruit and the bottom crust. With a sharp knife, trim the dough flush to the dish and crimp the edges (see page 210).

5 Unless you've added a pie funnel, cut three or four vents in the lid to let steam escape, and decorate with shapes cut from leftover pastry, rolled to about 2mm thick. Brush with beaten egg and sprinkle on the cinnamon and sugar for the topping.

6 Bake on the centre shelf of the oven for 30 minutes, then reduce the oven to 160°C/fan 140°C/gas mark 3 and cook for a further 15 minutes or until you can see juices bubbling through the steam vents or inside the funnel. Allow to cool before serving.

bright-red jam tarts

MAKES ABOUT 18 TARTS
*Equipment: 2 shallow bun tins;
1 x 7cm round pastry cutter*

1 quantity of Sweet Shortcrust
   Pastry (see page 215)
A little plain flour, for dusting
6 tbsp raspberry jam,
   or about ½ a pot
150g fresh raspberries

My beautiful five-year-old daughter, Kate, seems to have inherited my love of all things food-related. When asked 'How was school today?' her stock response is to simply recall the lunch menu. Together the two of us made this recipe, with Kate squashing the raspberries into the jam. We had so much fun that we had to include it in this book.

1 Make the sweet shortcrust pastry according to the method on page 215 and put it in the fridge to rest for 30 minutes.

2 On a lightly floured work surface, roll out the pastry to about 2mm thick. Cut out about eighteen 7cm circles and line the holes in the bun tins. Return to the fridge to chill for 30 minutes.

3 Preheat the oven to 190°C/fan 170°C/gas mark 5. When you are ready to fill the tarts, spoon a little jam into each pastry case – it should reach about three-quarters of the way up the sides. Add a raspberry or two to each case and submerge in the jam. It doesn't matter if a little fruit pokes out – it makes the tarts all the more beautiful.

4 Bake in the oven for 25 minutes or until the pastry has turned golden. Be very careful when you take the tarts out of the oven, as the jam will be very hot. Allow to cool for 30 minutes and serve for tea – if you can wait that long!

pretty white chocolate tarts

MAKES 6 TARTS
Equipment: 6 x 10cm round tartlet tins

1 quantity of Sweet Shortcrust
   Pastry (see page 215)
A little plain flour, for dusting
Edible rose petals, to decorate

For the filling:
175g good-quality white
   chocolate, broken up
150ml soured cream
150ml double cream

If you're careful melting the white chocolate, these are very easy and can be prepared up to 8 hours ahead. If you can't get rose petals, try just dusting the top heavily with cocoa powder.

1 Make the sweet shortcrust pastry according to the method on page 215 and put it in the fridge to rest for 30 minutes.

2 On a lightly floured work surface, roll out your pastry to about 2mm thick and cut out six 15cm circles. Carefully line the tins with them, trimming any excess, and put in the fridge for 30 minutes – this helps prevent shrinkage in the oven.

3 Preheat the oven to 200°C/fan 180°C/gas mark 6 and put a baking sheet in to heat up. Line each case with non-stick baking paper and fill with baking beans (see page 211). Place on the hot baking sheet in the oven and bake for 15 minutes, then remove the beans and paper and return to the oven for 8–10 minutes or until the pastry feels dry to the touch. Leave to cool completely.

4 Melt the chocolate in a heatproof bowl set over a pan of hot but not boiling water. Once melted, remove from the heat and stir in the soured cream. In a separate bowl, whip the double cream until it just forms soft peaks, then mix it gently into the white chocolate mixture. Spoon into the pastry cases and allow to set for at least 2 hours in the fridge. Decorate with rose petals to serve.

millefeuille 3 different ways

1 x 375g ready-rolled
all-butter puff pastry
A little plain flour, for dusting
1 medium egg, lightly whisked
2 tbsp icing sugar, plus extra
for dusting (optional)
Ingredients to fill the hearts:
see suggestions overleaf

Tip

To make your own template, use thin cardboard such as an empty cereal packet. Draw a heart shape 7cm across at its widest point and the same lengthways and cut round it with scissors.

Millefeuille is a French pastry made of many puff pastry layers. ('Mille' means a thousand, and 'feuille' means a leaf or sheet.) Making tiny pastries like this is a really pretty way to show off the buttery layers and the beautiful colour of the fillings. We've suggested hearts but you can make them any shape you like. This recipe is very simple to double up if you're expecting lots of guests, and the unfilled pastry shapes can be frozen once baked if you want to make a batch of them in advance.

1 Preheat the oven to 220°C/fan 200°C/gas mark 7 and line a baking sheet with non-stick baking paper.

2 Unroll the pastry on to a lightly floured surface and roll it out a bit thinner, to about 3mm thick. Using your cutter or template (see tip), cut out 12 hearts or whatever shape you fancy. Place on the prepared baking sheet and prick all over with a fork. Brush with beaten egg and bake in the oven for 10–12 minutes or until really crisp and golden.

3 Preheat the grill to medium-high. Dust the pastries with icing sugar, then place under the grill for a few seconds, watching them very carefully, until the sugar has caramelised.

4 Once cooled, use a sharp knife to split the pastry hearts into two layers, a top and a bottom. Now you are ready to make your filling.

recipe continues

Raspberry and Orange Curd
(Filling for 12 hearts)

Whisk 170ml double cream until just thickened. Mix in 3 tablespoons of Jaffa orange curd and a finely chopped ball of stem ginger. Spoon a layer of this orange cream over the bottom pastry layers, then add several fresh raspberries, pushing them gently into the cream, and a drizzle of ginger syrup (from the stem ginger jar). Top with the pastry hats. Sprinkle with icing sugar if you like.

Boozy Black Forest
(Filling for 12 hearts)

Make a chocolate custard by whisking 50g melted dark chocolate into 200g warmed ready-made custard. Leave in the fridge to thicken. Spoon a layer of the chocolate custard over the bottom pastry layers, then add a layer of black cherries in kirsch, along with a drizzle of the syrup and a good grating of dark chocolate. Top with the pastry hats and sprinkle with more grated chocolate if you like.

Rose Cream with Strawberries and Lime Zest
(Filling for 12 hearts)

Hull and quarter 200g strawberries, toss with the grated zest of 1 lime and 2 teaspoons of icing sugar and leave to macerate for 15 minutes. Whisk 170ml double cream to medium peaks with 1 tablespoon of icing sugar and 1 tablespoon of rose water. Spoon a layer of the rose cream over your bottom pastry layers, then add a layer of macerated strawberries. Top with the pastry hats. Finish with a dusting of icing sugar if you like.

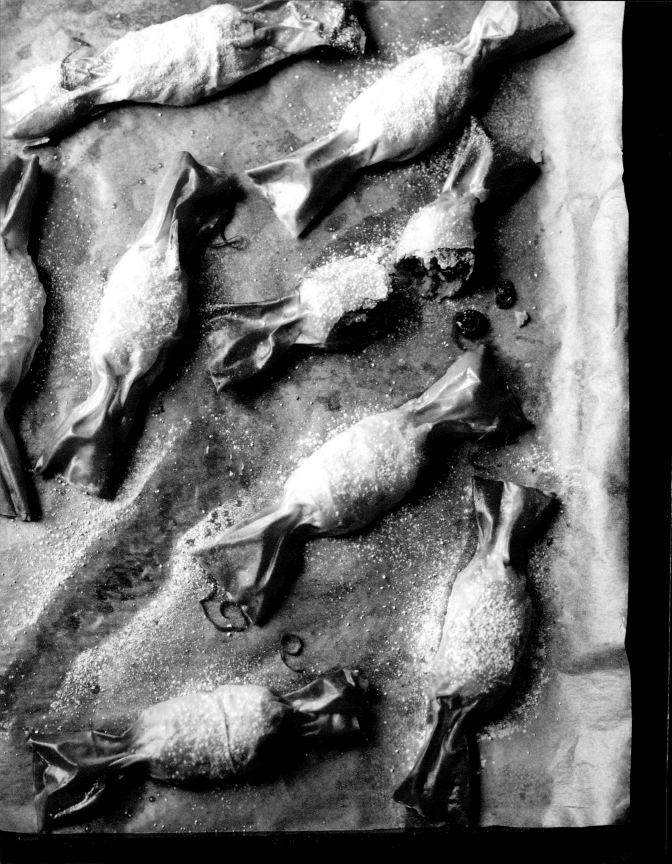

christmas cranberry crackers

MAKES 12
1 x 270g pack of filo pastry
50g butter, melted

For the filling:
60g dried cranberries
Juice and finely grated
  zest of 1 large orange
100g cream cheese
50g ground almonds
1 egg yolk
25g icing sugar, plus
  extra for dusting

Tip
For adults it's fun to serve
these with little cups of
espresso, or even a lightly
sweetened whisky cream
for indulgent dipping. ♡

These little crackers were inspired by my son Jack, who was born post-Christmas but pre-New Year, so he gets his own celebration before the tree has been taken down. You can vary the recipe as you wish – try adding spices, ginger, raisins or apricots.

1 Begin by soaking your cranberries in the fresh orange juice for 30 minutes. This will plump them up nicely.

2 Strain the cranberries and place in a large bowl, discarding any remaining juice. Add the rest of the filling ingredients and give the mixture a good stir. Chill for a minimum of 30 minutes before using.

3 When you are ready to assemble the crackers, preheat the oven to 180°C/fan 160°C/gas mark 4. Cut the stack of filo into 11cm x 18cm rectangles. Brush one filo rectangle with melted butter and top with a second piece of filo.

4 Dollop a good teaspoonful of filling into the centre of this rectangle and brush around the filling with a little more melted butter. Then wrap it up as if you were wrapping a sweet (not too tightly, as the filling will expand while cooking and burst the seams), squeezing the pastry together about 3cm in from each edge. Continue until all the filling and pastry is used up.

5 Arrange on a baking tray lined with non-stick baking paper, brush with a little more butter and bake for 15–20 minutes or until the filo is crispy and golden. Finish with a light dusting of icing sugar.

elderflower and raspberry baked apples

SERVES 6
Equipment: 1 x 8cm round fluted pastry cutter

320g ready-rolled all-butter
  puff pastry
A little plain flour, for dusting
100g fresh raspberries
120g good-quality raspberry jam
6 eating apples, Granny Smith
  or Cox's
100ml elderflower cordial
A knob of butter
1 medium egg, beaten
1–2 tbsp caster sugar
Vanilla ice cream, to serve

A quick apple pie scaled down, for those self-indulgent moments!

1 Preheat the oven to 200°C/fan 180°C/gas mark 6. Unroll the pastry on to a lightly floured work surface and cut out six circles with the cutter. Using the remaining pastry, cut out some little leaves and 'stalks' to decorate the pastry hats. Set these all aside.

2 Place the raspberries in a bowl, add the jam and gently stir so that all the raspberries are coated. Slice the bottom off each apple so that it can sit up straight, then remove the core and seeds (using either a sharp knife or an apple corer).

3 Place the apples on a lipped baking tray or in an ovenproof dish and fill the hole in the centre of each one with the raspberry mixture. Pour the elderflower cordial around the apples and add the butter.

4 Place a pastry hat on top of each apple, brush it with beaten egg, and decorate with your pastry leaves and stalks, sticking them on with beaten egg. Brush again with egg, then generously sprinkle with caster sugar.

5 Bake for 30–35 minutes or until the pastry is golden and crisp and the apples are soft and steaming. Serve each apple with a spoonful of the sticky red glaze and scoops of vanilla ice cream.

mochaccino tarts

MAKES 6 TARTS
*Equipment: 6 x 10cm round
fluted tartlet tins*

1 quantity of Chocolate
   Shortcrust Pastry (see page 215)
A little plain flour, for dusting
4 medium egg yolks, lightly beaten
50g golden caster sugar
150g dark chocolate (at least
   70% cocoa solids), broken up,
   plus extra for shavings
150ml espresso or strong
   coffee, cooled
50ml coffee liqueur,
   such as Kahlua
200ml double cream

To decorate:
400ml double cream
3 tbsp icing sugar

**My favourite way to finish a meal is with good coffee
and some rich dark chocolate. These satisfy both!**

1 Make the chocolate pastry according to the method on
page 215 and put it into the fridge to rest for 30 minutes.

2 On a lightly floured work surface, roll out the pastry to
about 2mm thick. Cut out six 15cm circles and line the tartlet
tins with them. Prick the bases with a fork and chill in the
fridge for 30 minutes.

3 Preheat the oven to 200°C/fan 180°C/gas mark 6 and put
a baking sheet in to heat up. Remove your pastry cases from
the fridge, line with non-stick baking paper and fill with
baking beans (see page 211). Bake on the hot baking sheet
for 15 minutes, then remove the paper and beans and return
to the oven for 5–8 minutes or until the pastry is dry and
completely cooked through. Remove the pastry cases from
the tins and set aside to cool completely.

4 Beat the egg yolks and caster sugar in a large bowl. Put the
chocolate, espresso, coffee liqueur and cream into a separate
bowl and stand it over a pan of barely simmering water until
melted. Gradually pour the chocolate mixture into the egg
mixture, whisking until well mixed, then transfer everything
to a clean pan.

5 Place over a gentle heat, stirring constantly with a wooden
spoon until the mixture thickens to form a custard. Remove
from the heat and pour through a sieve into a jug. Now
carefully pour into the pastry cases and place them in the
fridge for a minimum of 2 hours to set.

6 To decorate, whip the cream and icing sugar to soft peaks
and spoon on top of the tartlets, creating a nice swirl with
the back of your spoon. Decorate with chocolate shavings.

mini brown sugar banoffees

MAKES 15–20
LITTLE TARTS
*Equipment: 2 x shallow bun tins
or 1 x mini muffin tray*

For the pastry:
100g unsalted butter, softened
100g soft light brown sugar
2 medium eggs, beaten
325g plain flour, sifted,
   plus a little for dusting

To assemble:
300g condensed caramel
   (sometimes called dulce
   de leche, available in tins)
300ml extra-thick double cream
   or lightly whipped cream
1–2 ripe bananas, sliced
A little milk chocolate, for shaving
Cocoa powder, for dusting

These miniature banoffee pie-lets are sweet, crunchy and very, very delicious. We like to serve them after dinner, with coffee.

1 Here we like to use little bun tins that produce tarts about 2–3 bites in size. Cut out circles of non-stick baking paper to a size that will fit snugly into the bottom of your tins. Set aside.

2 To make the pastry, beat the butter and brown sugar using an electric whisk until pale (about 5 minutes), then slowly beat in the eggs. Add the flour and beat until just combined, then turn out on to a lightly floured work surface, form into a disc, wrap in clingfilm and chill for at least 30 minutes. Don't be tempted to use it sooner, as this pastry needs to rest.

3 When it's rested, roll out your pastry on a lightly floured work surface to about 2mm thick. Cut or stamp out circles to fit the bun tins or muffin tray, and line the holes with them (don't add the paper circles just yet). Chill for 30 minutes.

4 Preheat the oven to 180°C/fan 160°C/gas mark 4. Line each pastry case with a circle of non-stick baking paper and fill with baking beans (see page 211). Bake for 10 minutes, then remove the paper and beans and bake for another 5–7 minutes or until crisp. Remove the pastry cases from the tins and allow to cool completely.

5 Now simply assemble the pies. Fill each pastry case with condensed caramel and top with a little dollop of cream, a banana slice, shavings of chocolate and a light dusting of cocoa powder. Beautiful.

lemon posset pies

MAKES 6 TARTS

Equipment: 6 x 10cm shallow round tartlet tins

1 quantity of Sweet Shortcrust
    Pastry (see page 215)
A little plain flour, for dusting
300ml double cream
75g caster sugar
Finely grated zest of 1 lemon
2 tbsp lemon juice
100g fresh raspberries
1–2 tbsp chopped pistachios

Tip

Assemble these no earlier than the morning of the day they are to be eaten. This ensures that the pastry doesn't have a chance to soften and keeps the whole tart deliciously crisp!

I was taught to make lemon posset years ago by a chef who took particular pride in the teaching of traditional English puddings. He described posset as a luxurious recipe, and when you take a bite I think you'll agree. Instead of traditional ramekins, I've put the posset in buttery pastry cases and added a few fresh raspberries and chopped pistachios for even more luxuriousness.

1 Make the sweet shortcrust pastry according to the method on page 215 and put it in the fridge to rest for 30 minutes.

2 On a lightly floured work surface, roll out the pastry to about 2mm thick. Cut out six 15cm circles and line your tartlet tins with them. Prick the base of the pastry with a fork, then chill for 30 minutes.

3 Preheat the oven to 200°C/fan 180°C/gas mark 6 and put a baking sheet in to heat up. Line the tartlets with crumpled non-stick baking paper and fill with baking beans (see page 211). Bake on the hot baking sheet in the oven for 15 minutes, then remove the paper and beans and return to the oven for 8–10 minutes or until the edges are turning golden and the pastry is dry to the touch. Set aside to cool completely.

4 Put the cream, sugar and lemon zest into a small pan and place over a low heat, stirring constantly, until the sugar has completely dissolved. When bubbles start to form around the edges of the mixture, continue cooking gently without stirring for 2 minutes, but don't let the mixture boil. Remove from the heat and stir in the lemon juice. Finally, strain into a jug.

5 Remove the cooled tart cases from the tins. Place some raspberries in each one and pour the cooled (but not cold) lemon filling around them, letting some of the fruit poke out. Scatter with the chopped pistachios and put in the fridge for a minimum of 2 hours to set.

♡hearts full of fruit

MAKES 6 HEARTS
Equipment: 1 x 12cm and 1 x 9cm heart-shaped cutter (or make your own templates – see tip, below)

375g all-butter puff pastry
A little plain flour, for dusting
1 medium egg yolk, lightly beaten
Icing sugar, for dusting
175g white marzipan
A small selection of fruit: berries, freshly sliced nectarines, peeled and sliced eating apples
25g butter, melted
3 tbsp caster sugar

Tip
To make your own templates, use thin cardboard such as an empty cereal packet. Draw a heart shape 12cm across at its widest point and the same lengthways. Alongside it, draw a second heart shape, 1.5cm smaller all round than the first one (therefore 9cm across at its widest point). Cut out both shapes. ♡

Over the years these almondy hearts have been the answer to our search for a frugal, make-ahead pudding that looks completely beautiful. They can be pulled together almost entirely from the storecupboard, using a pack of puff pastry, some marzipan and any fruit you have in the bowl.

1 On a lightly floured work surface, roll out the puff pastry to 5–6mm thick. Using your larger cutter or template, cut out six heart shapes. Place on a baking sheet lined with non-stick baking paper and brush each one with beaten egg yolk.

2 Preheat the oven to 200°C/fan 180°C/gas mark 6. Dust your work surface with icing sugar and roll out the marzipan to about 4mm thick. Cut out six hearts, using the smaller cutter or template. Place your marzipan hearts on top of the pastry.

3 Arrange a handful of berries or sliced fruit on each marzipan heart. Brush the fruit with melted butter and sprinkle with the caster sugar.

4 Bake in the oven for 15–20 minutes or until the pastry is golden and the fruit has begun to caramelise. Serve warm.

easy
extras
and
perfect
pastry

sticky onions

SERVES 4 AS A SIDE DISH
Equipment: 4 x 10cm round tartlet tins

2 onions, about 150g each
80g caster sugar
A few sprigs of fresh thyme,
   leaves stripped
A little olive oil
200g all-butter puff pastry
Salt and freshly ground
   black pepper

Tip
To clean the caramel from
your pan, simply fill with
cold water and return to the
heat. Bring to the boil and
simmer for a few minutes.
This makes the residue
much easier to tackle!

Here, the humble onion is transformed into a sweet, caramelised side dish that makes an unusual but gorgeous accompaniment to our Beef Bourguignon Pie (page 51) or your Sunday roast.

1 Preheat the oven to 220°C/fan 200°C/gas mark 7. Prepare your tins by putting a small circle of non-stick baking paper in the base of each.

2 Peel the onions and slice in half, horizontally. Heat the sugar and 80ml of water in a small pan over a medium heat, without stirring, until the sugar completely dissolves. Turn up the heat, boil until the syrup turns golden, then immediately pour it into the lined tins – the syrup will solidify very quickly so immediately sprinkle in the thyme leaves and place an onion half, cut side down, into each tin. Season with salt and pepper and brush with a little olive oil.

3 Place the tins on a baking tray and bake for 25 minutes. Remove and allow to cool completely in the tins (leave the oven switched on).

4 Meanwhile, roll out the puff pastry to about 3mm thick and cut out four circles, just larger than your tins. Drape the pastry circles over the cooled onions and prick once or twice with a fork. Return to the hot oven for 20 minutes or until the pastry is golden brown.

5 Remove from the oven and, working quickly, carefully turn the tins over on to a baking tray. Remove the tins and serve the onions with a little extra seasoning.

easy extras
193

lemony baby potatoes

SERVES 6 AS A SIDE DISH

1kg baby new potatoes
4 tsp lemon juice
1 tsp Dijon mustard
2 tbsp olive oil
4 tbsp crème fraîche
6 spring onions, finely sliced
6 small cornichons, finely chopped
1 small bunch each of fresh
   flat-leaf parsley and dill,
   leaves chopped
Salt and freshly ground
   black pepper

Glorious new potatoes, lemon and crème fraîche add a touch of luxury to summer suppers. We suggest pairing with our little Smoked Salmon and Rocket Tarts (page 132).

1 Put the potatoes into a large pan of salted water, bring to the boil, then reduce the heat and simmer for 15 minutes or until tender. Drain and transfer to a large bowl.

2 Meanwhile, pour 2 teaspoons of the lemon juice into a small jam jar, add the mustard and oil, and season with salt and pepper. Put the lid on securely and give it a really good shake.

3 Stir the dressing into the warm potatoes and leave to cool for about 30 minutes so that the dressing can be absorbed. Add the crème fraîche, spring onions, cornichons, herbs and remaining lemon juice. Check the seasoning and serve.

spiced roasties

SERVES 6 AS A SIDE DISH

1kg baby new potatoes
1 tsp coriander seeds, crushed
1 tsp cumin seeds, crushed
3 tbsp olive oil
1 tbsp grainy mustard
1 small bunch of fresh flat-leaf
   parsley, leaves chopped

There's nothing quite like a roast potato to add some welcome crunch to your Sunday lunch. We like to serve these with the No-nonsense Steak and Ale Pie (page 47) – the touch of spice makes the whole meal sparkle!

1 Preheat the oven to 220°C/fan 200°C/gas mark 7. Bring a large pan of salted water to the boil. Add the potatoes and cook for 15 minutes or until tender. Drain well.

2 Tip the potatoes into a shallow roasting tin and crush them slightly with the back of a fork so that the skins just burst. Sprinkle with the coriander and cumin, drizzle over the oil and season with salt. Roast in the oven for 30 minutes or until crisp and golden. While they're still hot, add the mustard and parsley, and toss to coat.

rich onion gravy

MAKES 400ML
(SERVES 4)
A knob of butter
1 tbsp olive oil
1 large onion, sliced
2 tsp plain flour
75ml white wine
500ml good-quality hot
   vegetable stock
1 tsp redcurrant jelly
Salt and freshly ground
   black pepper

Not many sauces have a jug named after them; but such is the importance of gravy! We've used onion and a touch of redcurrant jelly to make this one extra-special.

1 Melt the butter and olive oil in a medium saucepan over a medium-low heat. Cook the onion, stirring occasionally (to stop it catching), for 15–20 minutes or until soft, golden and starting to caramelise.

2 Sprinkle in the flour, stir and cook for 1 minute. Pour in the white wine, allow to bubble until reduced and sticky, then add the stock. Bring to the boil, simmer for 10 minutes, then add the redcurrant jelly and stir to dissolve. Check the seasoning and add salt and pepper to taste. Serve piping hot.

petits pois and pancetta

SERVES 4 AS A SIDE DISH
A slosh of olive oil
350g cubed pancetta
300g frozen petits pois
¼ of a Savoy cabbage, tough
   outer leaves discarded and
   the rest finely shredded
A large knob of butter
A little freshly grated nutmeg
Salt and freshly ground
   black pepper

Combining peas, one of the sweetest vegetables, with salty pancetta creates a satisfying side dish full of flavour. We think this is best served with any of our chicken pie recipes or a good old lamb hotpot (see page 26).

1 Heat a slosh of oil in a large shallow pan over a high heat, then add the pancetta and sizzle for a few minutes or until beginning to turn golden. Add the petits pois, cabbage and a splash of water. Cover with a tightly fitting lid and cook over a medium heat for about 3 minutes.

2 Uncover the pan, add the butter, and season with salt, pepper and nutmeg. Serve immediately.

thrifty bubble and squeak cakes

Squeak!

SERVES 6 (MAKES 12 SMALL CAKES)

100g cavolo nero, spring greens, Savoy cabbage or kale, leaves shredded
600g cold mashed potato (see page 25 for method)
5 spring onions, white and green parts thinly sliced
70g feta cheese, crumbled
A little plain flour, for dusting
A large knob of butter
Salt and freshly ground black pepper

This classic combination is a great way to use up extra mash that's left over from your pie toppings! The cakes can be tarted up with a soft poached egg or rasher of crispy bacon on top.

1 Bring a large saucepan of salted water to the boil. Add the shredded greens and cook for 3 minutes or until tender, then drain and run under cold water to stop the cooking. Drain again, then dry the greens on kitchen paper.

2 Put your cold mash into a large bowl. Mix in the blanched greens, spring onions and feta, and season with salt and pepper to taste. Shape into 12 cakes (each about 1cm thick) and dust with a little flour.

3 Melt the butter in a large non-stick frying pan and fry the cakes over a medium heat for 2–3 minutes on each side or until golden and cooked through. Serve warm as a side dish, or topped with a poached egg for lunch.

braised fennel and baby leeks

SERVES 6 AS A SIDE DISH

2 fennel bulbs, trimmed
40g butter
100ml white wine
110g baby leeks
20g Parmesan cheese,
   finely grated
Salt and freshly ground
   black pepper

This is a delicate, pretty side dish that sits particularly nicely with our Hot-smoked Salmon Gougère (page 90).

1 Preheat the oven to 180°C/fan 160°C/gas mark 4. Cut the fennel bulbs into thick wedges, keeping the core intact.

2 Melt the butter in a shallow ovenproof pan on a medium heat. Place the fennel cut-side down in the butter. Season with salt and pepper and pour in the white wine. When bubbling, cover tightly with a lid or foil and bake in the oven for 30 minutes.

3 Remove from the oven, turn over the fennel bulbs and add the leeks. Put the lid back on and return to the oven for another 30 minutes or until really tender. Serve sprinkled with the Parmesan and a little more freshly ground black pepper.

garlicky green beans

SERVES 6 AS A SIDE DISH

280g green beans, tops
   trimmed, tails left on
40g butter
2 large garlic cloves,
   finely chopped
1 small red chilli, deseeded
   and finely chopped (optional)
4 spring onions, finely chopped
Salt and freshly ground
   black pepper

Green beans are too often cooked for a minute too many! Keep them bright green and crunchy and they will freshen up any plate. Serve with our Chinese Spiced Beef Pies or Pork and Apple Stroganoff Pie (pages 38 and 23).

1 Bring a small pan of salted water to the boil. Add the beans and cook for 3 minutes or until just tender, then drain well.

2 Melt the butter in a frying pan. Add the garlic and chilli (if using), cook for 30 seconds, then add the beans and toss to coat in the butter. Cook for a couple of minutes, then toss in the spring onions, give it all a good shake in the pan, and tip into a warm serving bowl. Season with salt and pepper.

spiced apple and onion chutney

MAKES 2 X 250ML JARS

450g eating apples
(6 small apples)
75g raisins or sultanas
1 small onion, finely chopped
160g demerara sugar
½ tsp coriander seeds, crushed
½ tsp smoked paprika
1 cinnamon stick
200ml cider vinegar
Salt

A jar or two of homemade chutney will have you feeling very domestic and is bound to impress guests. It's perfect served with warm, gooey wedges of our Giant Gruyère and Ham Sandwich (page 48).

1 Peel, core and chop the apples and place in a large saucepan with the raisins or sultanas, the onion, sugar and spices.

2 Add the cider vinegar, season generously with salt, and place over a low heat, stirring, until the sugar has dissolved. Cook for 45 minutes, stirring now and then. Cover with a lid halfway through the cooking time.

3 When ready, the chutney will have become thicker and the flavour will have mellowed. You should be able to draw your spoon through the middle and briefly see the base of the pan. Transfer the chutney into sterilised jars, seal and leave to cool. It keeps for about 3 months in the fridge.

fresh red salsa

SERVES 4–6
AS A SIDE DISH

300g cherry tomatoes, halved
1 large ripe avocado, peeled and
stone removed, roughly chopped
½ a red onion, finely chopped
1 green chilli, deseeded
and finely diced
1 small bunch of fresh coriander,
leaves chopped
Grated zest and juice of ½ a lime
½ tsp caster sugar
A generous glug of extra-virgin oil
Salt and freshly ground
black pepper

Not only is a fresh salsa very simple and swift to put together, it adds a certain vigour to other recipes. Dollop plenty on top of our Chilli Beef Pie (page 45) for the perfect combination.

1 Toss the cherry tomato halves and avocado pieces together in a large bowl. Add all the remaining ingredients and give everything a good stir.

2 Set aside for 10 minutes for the flavours to mingle, then check the seasoning and serve. This can be kept in the fridge for up to 24 hours (though the avocado may begin to go brown).

spicy chorizo beans

SERVES 6 AS A SIDE DISH
1 tbsp olive oil
1 onion, peeled and finely chopped
100g chorizo cooking sausage,
   chopped
1 large garlic clove, finely chopped
½ tsp dried chilli flakes
400g tin of chopped tomatoes
1 tbsp treacle
1 tsp cider vinegar
1 x 400g tin of haricot or
   cannellini beans, drained
   and rinsed
Salt and freshly ground
   black pepper

These beans are just as good on their own for breakfast as they are piled next to a grilled chicken breast for a warming supper. Comfort food with a kick!

1 Heat the oil in a large shallow pan over a medium heat and add the onion. Cook for 5 minutes to soften, then add the chorizo and cook for a further 5 minutes. Add the garlic and chilli flakes and cook for 1 minute more.

2 Tip in the tomatoes, treacle, vinegar and 250ml of water. Season well with salt and pepper, bring to a gentle bubble, and cook on a medium-low heat for 20 minutes, uncovered, until thickened.

3 Now add the beans and cook for another 15 minutes. Check the seasoning, adjust if necessary and serve warm.

fresh basil pesto

MAKES 250ML
1 garlic clove
2 tbsp pine nuts, toasted
60g fresh basil leaves
20g Parmesan cheese,
   finely grated
Juice of ½ a lemon
120ml extra-virgin olive oil
Salt and freshly ground
   black pepper

It is not just Italians who are passionate about pesto. Stir through pasta, add to a dressing or pop a jar of it on the table, alongside the mustard, to complement a warm chicken pie or steaming sausage roll.

1 In the small bowl of a food processor, or using a pestle and mortar, whiz or pound the garlic clove with a pinch of salt. Add the toasted pine nuts and coarsely grind. Then add the basil leaves and keep pounding to a textured paste.

2 Transfer to a bowl and stir in all the remaining ingredients. Check the seasoning, adding more salt and pepper to taste. This keeps for up to a week, covered, in the fridge.

raw cabbage slaw

SERVES 6 AS A SIDE DISH
4 rashers of rindless streaky
   bacon, cut into lardons
¼ of a red cabbage
¼ of a white cabbage
1 small red onion, very finely sliced
1 red-skinned apple,
   cored and finely sliced
35g pecan nuts, roughly chopped
Mixed fresh herbs, chopped
   (e.g. mint, dill, flat-leaf parsley)

For the dressing:
6 tbsp crème fraîche
1 tbsp lemon juice
1 tbsp extra-virgin olive oil
2 tsp Dijon mustard
Salt and freshly ground
   black pepper

Cabbage has long been the victim of bad press, often dismissed as soggy and bland. But this recipe bucks the trend. It's fresh and crisp, with a tart, creamy dressing. Try it alongside our Sausage and Bean Pie (page 15).

1 Fry the bacon in a dry frying pan on a medium-high heat until crisp. Quarter, core and finely shred the red and white cabbage. Put into a large bowl with the red onion, apple, cooked bacon and pecan nuts.

2 Whisk together the dressing ingredients, seasoning with salt and pepper to taste. Pour the dressing into the bowl with the cabbage mixture, add the herbs and toss to coat. Serve immediately.

spiced tomato sauce

2 tbsp olive oil
2 red onions, peeled and chopped
2 large garlic cloves, chopped
½ tsp fennel seeds
1 tsp cumin seeds
2 tsp ground coriander
2 x 400g tins of chopped tomatoes
A pinch of salt
1 tbsp soft brown sugar

Homemade tomato sauce is a great all-rounder, which can always be put to good use. It's a key ingredient in many of the pie fillings throughout this book, and can also be used on pizza or simply stirred through pasta.

1 Heat the olive oil in a large shallow pan over a gentle heat. Add the onions and cook them for 5 minutes to soften. Add the garlic and spices to the pan, and cook, stirring, for a couple more minutes.

2 Pour over the tomatoes and add the salt and sugar. Stir well, then simmer gently, uncovered, for about 30 minutes or until slightly syrupy in consistency. The sauce can be kept, covered, in the fridge for up to a week.

puff pastry croutons

MAKES ABOUT 24

A little plain flour, for dusting
200g all-butter puff pastry
30g Parmesan cheese, finely grated
1 medium egg, lightly beaten

The ultimate in kitchen recycling – leftover pastry and leftover cheese baked together to create something wonderful that will perk up salads and soups in seconds.

1 Preheat the oven to 220°C/fan 200°C/gas mark 7. On a lightly floured work surface, roll out the pastry to about 4mm thick. Sprinkle half the Parmesan over one half of the pastry, then fold the other half over the top to enclose the cheese. Roll out the pastry again. Brush the top with beaten egg and sprinkle with the remaining Parmesan.

2 Cut into 2cm squares (or stamp out little heart shapes) and place on a baking sheet lined with non-stick baking paper. Bake for 12–15 minutes or until crisp and golden. Toss into a salad or scatter over bowls of steaming soup. Stored in an airtight container, these will keep for up to a week.

easy extras

roasted beetroot with pears and goat's cheese

SERVES 6 AS A SIDE DISH

6 medium uncooked beetroots
4 tbsp extra-virgin olive oil
1 tbsp cider vinegar
1 tsp Dijon mustard
3 sprigs of fresh thyme,
   leaves stripped
3 pears, such as Williams,
   cored and cut into wedges
   (leave the skin intact)
75g walnut halves, toasted
1 small bunch of fresh flat-leaf
   parsley, leaves chopped
150g ripe soft goat's cheese,
   cut into pieces
Salt and freshly ground
   black pepper

Beetroot recipes so often look beautiful and this is no exception. The colours and flavours sit naturally together in a sophisticated salad that can be eaten on its own or is perfect with our Wintry Pizza Pie (page 18).

1 Preheat the oven to 200°C/fan 180°C/gas mark 6.

2 Peel the beetroots (wearing rubber gloves to avoid staining your hands) and place on a large sheet of foil. Drizzle with 1 tablespoon of the oil and season with salt and pepper.

3 Scrunch up the foil into a parcel and roast on a baking tray in the oven for 1 hour. Test to see if they are cooked with the tip of a sharp knife – it should go in really easily. If not, return to the oven until tender. Remove, and cut into wedges.

4 Make a dressing by pouring the remaining oil into a jam jar with the vinegar, mustard and thyme. Season with salt and pepper, put a lid on the jar, then give it a really good shake.

5 Pour the dressing over the beetroot wedges while they are still warm and leave for 10 minutes. Add the pears, walnuts and parsley and mix gently. Heap on to a serving plate and crumble or scatter the goat's cheese over the top.

roasted butternut squash wedges

SERVES 6 AS A SIDE DISH

1 large butternut squash
4 sprigs of fresh rosemary
2–3 tbsp olive oil
1 bulb whole garlic, split
    into cloves and bruised
    (press with the side of
    a knife to crack the skins)
2 sprigs of fresh oregano,
    leaves stripped and chopped
Salt and freshly ground
    black pepper

With its buttery flesh and papery skin, squash responds really well to being roasted and the resulting texture is unbeatable. These wedges are good served with our Venison Sausage Pies (page 19). Roast a little extra and you'll have a gorgeous standby ingredient to throw into a salad or pop in a pitta for tomorrow's lunch.

1 Preheat the oven to 220°C/fan 200°C/gas mark 7.

2 Halve the squash and remove the seeds, leaving the skin on, then cut it into wedges (approximately 2cm thick). Scatter over a large shallow ovenproof dish or roasting tin. Add the rosemary sprigs, drizzle with the oil and season with salt and pepper. Toss to coat, then add the bruised garlic to the tin.

3 Roast in the oven for 30–40 minutes until the squash is tender and starting to caramelise. Sprinkle over the oregano and roast for 5 minutes more. Season again and serve.

perfect pastry

Making your own pastry is both rewarding and therapeutic. On the next few pages are recipes for savoury shortcrust pastry plus some variations and twists. Remember, a few important things hold true whatever type of pastry you are making: always measure your ingredients accurately, keep everything as cold as possible and don't be tempted to handle the pastry too much or it can become tough and chewy. Most of all, just have a go and don't panic.

a few tips for handling pastry

Resting your pastry

Once you have made your pastry, it's really important to let it sit in the fridge for at least 30 minutes. This allows the pastry to relax, which helps reduce any shrinking when it's in the oven, as well as making it firmer and easier to roll. Please don't be tempted to bypass this stage.

Rolling, lining and trimming

After your pastry has relaxed in the fridge, allow 10 minutes for it to 'warm up' at room temperature before you begin rolling. This also applies to blocks of ready-made pastry bought from the supermarket.

Dust your work surface and rolling pin lightly with flour to prevent the pastry sticking and tearing, then begin to roll it out, rolling away from yourself and in just one direction at a time. The goal is to flatten the pastry rather than stretch it, so turn it frequently – this helps to achieve an even thickness all over. Remember to turn the pastry, not your body!

If the pastry sticks to the work surface, loosen by sliding a palette knife underneath.

For really delicate pastries such as sweet ones made with lots of butter and sugar, it's best to roll between sheets of non-stick baking paper.

If your rolled-out pastry is covered in excess flour, lightly flick a dry pastry brush over the top and bottom to remove it. Then gently ease the pastry into the tin or pie dish, taking care not to stretch the pastry.

Once you've lined your tart tin or pie dish, you can roll a rolling pin across the top of the tin to loosen any excess pastry at the sides. Then use a small sharp knife to cut away this excess, working around the sides in sweeping downward strokes, turning the tin as you go. This is easiest if you hold the tin at eye level.

Now gently prick the base of the pastry with a fork. This helps release trapped air so that it stays flat while baking. But try not to prick all the way through the base or your filling may escape later on!

Crimping

Crimping is a method used to seal the pastry around the edge of your pie dish or tin. It also looks very nice! The easiest way to crimp is to pinch the edges of the pastry between your thumb and forefinger, or you can press into the pastry with the prongs of a fork or even the back of a teaspoon. Make sure to pinch or press firmly – anything too subtle will just disappear while baking.

Knocking up

Knocking up is a technique sometimes used for puff pastry – it helps loosen the layers of pastry and let air get in between them, which encourages the pastry to puff up and makes the pie look glorious. To do this, hold the blade of a very sharp knife horizontally to the edge of your raw pastry case and, with your other hand, press down gently on the edge of the pastry next to the knife. Tap gently into the edge of the pastry all the way round the pie, then brush the top of the pie with beaten egg – trying really hard not to let any egg drip down on to the knocked-up sides as it will stop them separating and puffing up.

Decorating and glazing

Decorating the top of your pie with pastry shapes is a great way to use up scraps and give a hint as to what's inside. Gather up your scraps of leftover pastry and roll out to about 2mm thick. Use pastry cutters or go freestyle to make pretty decorations such as leaves, apples, fishes, hearts and stars. Arrange over the top of your pie lid and secure in place with a little beaten egg. If your decorations are especially thick, you might need to add a few extra minutes to the baking time.

At Higgidy, we love to add a heavy glaze, to give our pies a gorgeous golden sheen. Experiment with lightly beaten egg, single cream or whole milk. For a really intense sheen and a rich golden colour, you can double-glaze. It's exactly that – brush the pie lid with beaten egg and then brush it again. Or for a super-glossy finish, add a single egg yolk to your beaten-egg mixture.

After glazing you can sprinkle the top of your pie with spices, herbs, grated cheese, nuts, seeds or sugar. Our favourite toppings are dried chilli flakes, caraway or black onion seeds, ground polenta, pink peppercorns and golden granulated sugar.

Blind baking

You may have wondered what this term means. Put simply, it's the process of baking an empty pastry case before adding a filling. This is necessary when the pastry takes longer to cook than the filling, so blind baking gives it a headstart. It also helps prevent the pastry becoming soggy once the filling is added.

To blind bake your pastry case, make sure you have pricked the base several times with a fork, then line with a circle of non-stick baking paper wide enough to come up the sides. Fill with a generous layer of ceramic baking beans, though not so full it's at risk of overflowing. (If you don't have ceramic beans, dried beans or chickpeas work equally well. You can re-use them too – let them cool down completely, then store in a jar.) The beans provide support for the sides and weigh down the empty base so it doesn't rise up while baking. Then bake the pastry case as instructed in the recipe.

If you find a few cracks or holes after the case is baked, don't panic. Just take a bit of leftover raw pastry and patch up the holes, then brush with beaten egg and soldier on! These little bits of raw pastry will bake with the filling.

A little note about filo, puff and other types of pastry

You will notice we've not given recipes for making puff pastry or filo pastry from scratch. This is because both are very fiddly and time-consuming to make, so we recommend you use shop-bought. For puff pastry, the all-butter variety tastes the nicest and puffs up beautifully into crispy layers.

A few recipes in this book call for more complicated pastry techniques, such as the Hot-smoked Salmon Gougère on page 90, which involves choux pastry, or the Wonderful Wedding Pie on page 79–80, which is made with hot-water crust pastry. For these, you'll find detailed instructions in the recipe itself, but the basic principles still apply – measuring carefully, keeping the pastry cold, allowing it time to rest, and not over-handling.

perfect pastry

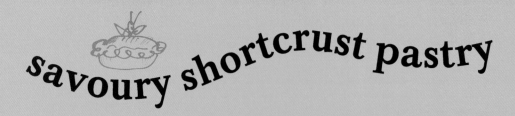

savoury shortcrust pastry

MAKES 350G

200g plain flour
A generous pinch of salt
100g butter, well chilled
   and cut into small cubes
30g Parmesan cheese,
   grated (optional)
1 medium egg yolk, beaten
About 3 tbsp ice-cold water

Traditional shortcrust pastry is made up of two parts plain flour to one part fat (such as butter or lard), plus a tiny amount of water. At Higgidy, we've had lots of practice making shortcrust pastry, so here is our trusted recipe, which is delicious and easy to handle. For the ultimate savoury flavour, we add cheese. This makes it taste great and gives the pastry a gorgeous golden colour when baked, but you can omit this if you prefer a more traditional approach. For a richer pastry you can add a touch more butter and an egg yolk, or for a shorter, silkier texture you can use a combination of butter and lard. The pastry can be made easily by hand or in a food processor.

How it's done – by hand

Sift the flour and salt into a large mixing bowl. Add the butter cubes and use your fingertips and thumbs to lightly rub it into the flour until the mixture resembles breadcrumbs. Add the Parmesan (if using) and rub again until the cheese is mixed in evenly. Now add the beaten egg yolk and water, and use a round-bladed knife to combine the wet ingredients with the dry until the pastry comes together. Gather it up with your hands and knead very briefly into a ball on a lightly floured surface. Try not to handle it too much at this stage, or the fat will get warm and the pastry will become tricky to use and may turn out tough and chewy. Wrap in clingfilm and chill for 30 minutes before use.

How it's done – in a food processor

Making shortcrust pastry in a food processor takes just minutes. Process the flour, butter and cheese (if using) until the mixture resembles breadcrumbs. Add the egg yolk beaten with the ice-cold water. Pulse until the mixture just comes together to form a dough, adding a tiny bit more water if you think it's needed. Wrap in clingfilm and chill for 30 minutes.

If you're feeling adventurous...

Once you've mastered the basics of shortcrust pastry you can experiment with the sweet and gluten-free versions overleaf, and with adding extra flavours such as nuts, herbs or seeds – see suggestions below. Stir in once the mixture resembles fine breadcrumbs, just before you add the egg yolk and water. Be aware that some additions, such as moist herbs or oily nuts, can make the pastry harder to handle. Try the following:

* A tablespoon of finely chopped fresh herbs – woody herbs such as thyme, rosemary and oregano work best. Avoid wetter herbs like chives or parsley, and remember to remove any stalks before chopping.

* A couple of teaspoons of seeds, such as sesame, poppy, black onion or caraway. These add flavour and texture to the pastry. The darker-coloured seeds look really pretty too.

* Spices, such as a pinch of saffron threads, paprika or chilli flakes. These taste delicious and give the pastry a beautiful colour.

* 40–50g finely chopped walnuts, pecans or hazelnuts. You can add these to both savoury and sweet shortcrust pastry.

* Grated lemon, lime or orange zest, to give sweet shortcrust pastry some zing. Use your finest grater, to achieve the best distribution through the pastry, and add the zest to the flour before rubbing in the butter.

sweet shortcrust pastry

MAKES 500G

250g plain flour, plus a
little for dusting
50g icing sugar
A pinch of salt
135g butter, well chilled
and cut into small cubes
1 medium egg, beaten
2–3 tbsp ice-cold water
or whole milk

This simple sweetened shortcrust is great for any fresh fruit pie or sweet deep-filled tart. See page 213 for extra ingredients you can add to make it even more delicious.

Sift the flour, icing sugar and salt into a large bowl or a food processor. Add the butter cubes and lightly rub in with your fingertips or pulse until the mixture resembles breadcrumbs. Add the beaten egg and cold water or milk and use a round-bladed knife or pulse to combine the ingredients until the pastry comes together, adding a tiny bit more liquid if needed. Gather it up with your hands and knead very briefly into a ball on a lightly floured surface. Try not to handle it too much at this stage, or the fat will get warm and the pastry will become tricky to use and may turn out tough and chewy. Wrap in clingfilm and chill for 30 minutes before use.

chocolate shortcrust pastry

MAKES 375G

175g plain flour, plus
a little for dusting
1 tbsp good-quality cocoa powder
50g icing sugar
100g unsalted butter, chilled
and cut into small cubes
1 medium egg yolk, beaten
1–2 tbsp ice-cold water

It's fun to complement a rich chocolate filling with chocolate pastry. It's also lovely blind-baked and filled with fresh berries and a warm berry jam glaze.

Sift the flour, cocoa powder and icing sugar into a large bowl or a food processor and rub in or process with the butter until the mixture resembles breadcrumbs. Add the beaten egg yolk and ice-cold water, then stir or pulse just enough to bring the pastry together. Turn out on to a lightly floured work surface and knead lightly until smooth. Try not to handle too much at this stage or the fat will get warm and the pastry may turn out tough and chewy. Wrap in clingfilm and chill for 30 minutes before use.

gluten-free shortcrust pastry

MAKES 400G

150g potato flour, plus
  a little for dusting
65g fine-ground polenta
1 tsp xanthan gum
A pinch of salt
140g butter, well chilled
  and cut into small cubes
1 medium egg, beaten
1 tbsp ice-cold water (optional)

Gluten is a protein found in cereals such as wheat, and therefore in most types of flour. When mixed with water it forms stretchy strands that give pastry its consistency and make it suitable for rolling, cutting and lining tins or pie dishes. So the big challenge with gluten-free pastry is in achieving the same consistency as with a wheat-based one. While writing this book we've experimented with different flours and also xanthan gum, a magic white powder (!) that helps make the pastry stretchy. You'll find it in the baking aisle of the supermarket. After lots of trial and error, we think this recipe works pretty well. It's quite delicate so is best made by hand.

1 Put the potato flour, polenta, xanthan gum and salt into a large bowl. Add the butter cubes to the bowl and, using your fingertips and thumbs, lightly rub together until the mixture resembles breadcrumbs.

2 Now add the beaten egg and use a round-bladed knife to combine with the dry ingredients until the pastry comes together. You might need a splash of ice-cold water to bring it together. Using your hands, gather it up and knead very briefly on a surface lightly dusted with potato flour. Form into a ball. Try not to handle it too much at this stage, or the fat will get warm and the pastry will become tricky to use and may turn out tough and chewy. Wrap in clingfilm and chill for 30 minutes before use.

3 Roll and line according to the recipe you are following, but to bake blind (see page 211) with gluten-free pastry, you need to reduce the oven temperature by 10°C (or by one gas mark) and the cooking time by 5 minutes.

quick soured cream pastry

MAKES 400G

175g plain flour, plus
   a little for dusting
A tiny pinch of salt
150g butter, well chilled
   and cut into small cubes
90ml soured cream

This lovely pastry is super-quick to make and has a very soft texture. As long as you don't over-mix, it's almost foolproof. Try adding fresh herbs, such as thyme or oregano.

Sift the flour and salt into a large bowl or food processor and add the butter. Rub in with your fingertips or pulse until the mixture resembles breadcrumbs. Add the soured cream and stir or pulse for 2–3 seconds, or until just mixed. Bring together on a lightly floured surface and shape into a flat disc, then wrap in clingfilm and chill for 30 minutes before use.

savoury croustade pastry

MAKES 350G

200g plain flour, plus
   a little for dusting
A generous pinch of salt
75g butter, well chilled
   and cut into small cubes
50g mature Cheddar
   cheese, finely grated
1 medium egg, beaten
1–2 tbsp ice-cold water

Try making this rich, cheesy pastry for any of our croustades or freeform pies. The cheese gives it a lovely nutty brown colour when baked, and it tastes delicious!

Sift the flour and salt into a large bowl or a food processor, add the butter cubes and rub in with your fingertips or pulse until the mixture resembles breadcrumbs. Add the grated Cheddar, and stir or pulse until the cheese is just mixed in. Add the beaten egg and a few splashes of ice-cold water and mix or pulse just enough to bring the pastry together. Turn out on to a lightly floured work surface and knead lightly until smooth. Try not to handle too much or the fat will get warm and the pastry may turn out tough and chewy. Wrap in clingfilm and chill for 30 minutes before use.

index

a recipe of thanks ♡

MAKES 1 DELICIOUS COOKBOOK

A passionate Jane
One stylish Jenny
A very organised Ione
Spoonfuls of inspiration from Dan
Two large bunches of creative
    energy from Lucy and Georgina
Heaps of patience from Joanna
Tons of talent from Tamzin
    and Mark
To decorate: a generous
    sprinkling of fresh thinking
    from Alex and Emma

1 Take one adventurous idea. Add a passionate proposal and a brilliant Jane Turnbull, then leave for a few weeks to marinate.

2 Next, mix with Jenny and Ione, the talented team at Quercus. Allow to simmer gently for several months while waistlines begin to develop.

3 Drink lots of coffee and eat plenty of pie with Lucy O'Reilly, Georgina Fuggle and Joanna Stanic. Test and write over 100 recipes before repeating the process.

4 Throw Emma and Alex from Smith & Gilmour into the pie, mix with spice and vigour before leaving to rest overnight.

5 Preheat the oven to a high heat and add Dan Jones, Andrew Smith and a very good camera. Make all of the recipes all over again. Line your tin carefully with props from Tamzin Ferdinando and illustrations from Mark Beech and bake until golden.

6 Serve straight from the oven with lashings of help from the whole Higgidy team!

about camilla and higgidy

Camilla Stephens began making pies in 2003, having trained as a cook at Leiths School of Food and Wine. She worked for a time as head of food development for Starbucks UK, but as Starbucks expanded, Camilla decided to follow her dreams and start her own food business. And so Higgidy was born. Camilla began experimenting with individually crafted pies full of tasty ingredients. While she didn't intend to reinvent pies, she was determined to revive them and make them appealing to women as well as men, so she took traditional recipes and gave them a twist. She didn't realise it at the time, but this became key to the evolution of the Higgidy brand. Camilla's recipes have seen Higgidy become one of the fastest-growing food companies in the UK, with their lovingly made gourmet pies and quiches now stocked in most of Britain's major supermarkets. Camilla is married to James and they have two children, Kate and Jack, who also love to cook. This is her first cookbook.

Quercus Editions Ltd, 55 Baker Street
7th Floor, South Block, London W1U 8EW

First published in 2013

A catalogue record of this book is available from the British Library

ISBN 978 1 78206 289 9

Publishing Director: Jenny Heller
Editor: Ione Walder
Design, layout and cover: Smith & Gilmour

Food styling: Lucy O'Reilly and Georgina Fuggle
Prop styling: Tamzin Ferdinando
Copy-editing: Annie Lee

Printed and bound in China

10 9 8 7 6 5 4 3